MAN IN ESTRANGEMENT

guyton b. hammond   MAN

A Comparison
of the Thought of

paul tillich
and
erich fromm

IN ESTRANGEMENT

§

1965, Vanderbilt University Press
Nashville, Tennessee

To Bruce, who someday will read it

contents

fOREWORD

I T is both a pleasure
and an honor to be asked to help introduce Guyton B. Hammond's book "Man in Estrangement" to the theological public.
A second reading of the manuscript has convinced me that this
is a most important volume, one which will be of inestimable
help to all students of contemporary thought. For Professor
Hammond has illumined for us not only one of the most pervasive and significant of modern themes, the subject of alienation or estrangement, but he has done so in terms of two of the
most creative thinkers of our time, the psychological and social
analyst Erich Fromm and the philosopher-theologian Paul Tillich.

The author traces the development of the idea of alienation
from its inception with Hegel through its various transformations
in Feuerbach, Marx, Freud, and the modern existentialists; then
he shows how the same general concept from out of this common
background is treated in Fromm in terms of psychological and
social thought and by Tillich in terms of a theologically oriented
ontology. The clarification of this "existentialist" tradition and
of the thought about man of Fromm, one of the most prominent
present representatives of that tradition, alone would have made
the book important.

It is, however, its interpretation of Tillich that gives this volume its greatest value. Among the many books and articles that
have recently appeared on Tillich, few have done much more
than state the basic concepts of the system and then criticize them
from one point of view or another. Professor Hammond, on the

contrary, has sought not only to state but also to *interpret* Tillich's theology, to find its most fundamental and thus often not obvious notions and their interrelationships, and to understand the problem of estrangement in this light.

Thus, for example, after outlining as have many others the familiar method of "correlation," he proceeds to explore how the "questioning" elements therein actually work by comparing the secularist Fromm's analysis of man's estrangement with the theologian Tillich's view of our predicament. In the course of this comparision, where the difference between the "question" as raised by a social psychologist and the question as raised by a theologian become obvious, Professor Hammond illuminates more than any previous commentator the actual relations in Tillich's system between philosophical analyses and theological answers.

Most of all, in tracing out the concept of estrangement in Tillich, Professor Hammond finds he has to explore in depth the concepts of finite freedom, creation and the creative activity of God. In the process he presents us with a radically new but, in my view, quite correct interpretation of the concept of God in Tillich. As he amply demonstrates, this concept is characterized more by the dynamic notion of "life" than it is by the more static notion of "being itself," with the result that the inner life of God is shown for the first time to be the key to the difficult notions of creativity, finitude, self-transcendence, and even the "fall" into existence. Thus a decisively new interpretation of Tillich is here presented, which clarifies many of the older puzzles in Tillichiana, especially the intimate relations of being and process, of creation and fall, of pantheism and theism, and the significant question of the goodness and permanence of finitude as such. I regard this as at once the most creative and authoritative interpretation of Tillich I have encountered, and I thus regard this volume to be of great interest to all those with theological and philosophical concerns.

LANGDON GILKEY

June 1965
The Divinity School
The University of Chicago

pReface

WHEN the last revision has been made and the manuscript must stand, imperfect but completed, it is appropriate to recall those who helped give it such virtues as it does possess. I should, therefore, like to express my appreciation to three advisers who gave wise counsel: professors Roger L. Shinn, now of Union Theological Seminary, Gordon D. Kaufman, now of Harvard Divinity School, and Langdon B. Gilkey, now of the University of Chicago Divinity School. I am also grateful for the suggestions of Professor James E. Sellers of the Vanderbilt Divinity School. For the stimulation of conversation with friends, and especially for my wife's encouragement, I must express my thanks as well.

Although my thinking has been shaped by the Christian perspective, the structure of the book reflects my conviction that Christian wisdom concerning man cannot remain in "splendid isolation" but must renew its strength through dialogue with the best secular wisdom which the modern period offers. This dialogue cannot occur in general; it must take place among those who share enough common ground to speak intelligibly to one another. The mere juxtaposition of radically different views proves nothing. Insight emerges when thinkers representing different traditions converge upon a central concept, or when they are found to draw different conclusions from common assumptions.

It is hoped that this study relating Paul Tillich and Erich Fromm is an example of that dialogue which can be genuinely productive. The two men share a common tradition in some respects; as a result, their differences become the more illuminating. Also, their convergence from different directions upon the concept of estrangement appears to be significant. There is no attempt here to refute one by means of the other. Rather, my central purpose is to look through the eyes of both at that complex, mysterious entity which is human nature.

A reader desiring only a general introduction to the thought of the two men without the detailed analysis of estrangement and reconciliation may choose to omit Chapters Five, Six, Ten, and Eleven.

GUYTON B. HAMMOND

Blacksburg, Virginia
April 1965

MAN IN ESTRANGEMENT

I

introduction

Setting the Problem S TUDIES of human
nature have been enriched in recent years by a renewal of com-
munications between religious and secular evaluations of the
human condition. In philosophy, the dialogue between theologians and the existentialists has been most interesting; in the
area of the sciences of man, perhaps the conversations between
theologians and the various schools of psychoanalysis have
proved most rewarding. Although purists on both sides of these
discussions fear the intrusion of alien elements, such dialogues
promise to add significantly to man's self-understanding.

From the side of Christian theology, one of the foremost
contributors has been Paul Tillich. The main thrust of Tillich's
body of writings has been the effort to relate the Christian concept of man to interpretations of the human situation produced
by modern culture. Indeed, Tillich has incorporated the principle
of dialogue into a formal theological method, the "method of
correlation." This methodological structure, upon which Tillich's
systematic theology rests, represents an attempt to "correlate"
certain contemporary analyses of man's predicament with the
"answers" provided by "the symbols used in the Christian message." According to Tillich, the positive content of the Christian
faith, though not derivable from an analysis of the human situation, must be formulated in a way that will provide answers to
the questions actually raised in man's contemporary self-
analysis.

3

The implementation of Tillich's method raises many issues of philosophical and theological interest. This study proposes to analyze the method of correlation through its application—to perform a concrete experiment in correlation. As the second party in the dialogue, representing a nontheological concept of man, Erich Fromm has been selected. Fromm's analysis of man, presented in a series of studies approaching systematic structure, incorporates psychoanalytical and sociological insights into a viewpoint which stands in the tradition of naturalistic humanism. He seeks to combine the "sciences of man" with a philosophical perspective that has its roots in Renaissance, Enlightenment, and nineteenth-century existentialist sources. Thus his work serves to represent effectively certain major currents of modern thought concerning man. Also, Fromm's interest in religious phenomena makes him an important contributor to the dialogue which we are investigating.

A study relating Tillich and Fromm proves especially rewarding because of certain similarities in their thought. These similarities, which will be examined in detail as the study proceeds, set into sharper relief the question of irreducible differences between a theistic and a nontheistic evaluation of man and the human predicament. Our study will be given structure, then, by our effort to discover what might actually be involved in a concrete correlation of Fromm's analysis of man with the "Christian message" as Tillich formulates it. Our final purpose, however, is to engage the two men in a critical dialogue—a dialogue which will illuminate their concepts, and, hopefully, through these concepts man himself, the ultimate object of our study.

The Concept of Estrangement

A careful examination of the method of correlation reveals that it is inseparable from a particular content which Tillich finds in many otherwise diverse analyses of human existence. This recurrent theme is the recognition of human "estrangement," of man's separation or "alienation" from something with which he ought to be united. As our study will show, the method of correlation assumes that the fundamental discovery of modern man's self-analysis is the fact of his estrangement. No matter whether this concept possesses the universal significance which Tillich attributes to it, one cannot deny that it has figured importantly in the literature concerning modern man. We find that the concept of alienation occupies a central place in Fromm's analysis of man. Therefore, the effort to correlate the thought of Fromm and Tillich becomes, on the substantive level, a comparison of two concepts of estrangement or alienation, the one naturalistic, the other theological. We shall discover that correlation in Tillich's sense is actually a transformation of nontheistic ideas of estrangement. This concept is consequently the center of our own analysis. Before we proceed any further it will be helpful to suggest something of the philosophical background, the "family tree," from which this concept emerges.

Tillich and Fromm agree in viewing estrangement and alienation as synonymous translations of the German *Entfremdung* (Tillich prefers the former, Fromm the latter translation). Three significant denotations of alienation can be distinguished: (1) in property relations, "the transfer of the title to property by one person to another"; (2) in personal relations, "a withdrawing or an estrangement, as of feeling or the affections"; (3) in psychology, "a deprivation, or partial deprivation of mental faculties; derangement; insanity."[1]

In modern philosophical usage, the origin of the term "estrangement" is generally attributed to G. W. F. Hegel (1770–1831). The concept has a possible application in many areas. F. H. Heinemann refers to alienation as a "multidimensional phenomenon," citing the psychological, the psychopathological, the sociological, the religious, and the metaphysical dimensions.[2] Something of the complexity of the idea can be suggested here by a brief synopsis of Hegel's formulations and

1. *The Century Dictionary,* ed. William Dwight Whitney.
2. F. H. Heinemann, *Existentialism and the Modern Predicament,* pp. 9–10.

of the reactions against Hegel's approach by Ludwig Feuerbach and Karl Marx. In this study, the concepts of estrangement formulated by Tillich and Fromm will be viewed against the background of these three philosophers.[3]

An analysis of estrangement appears implicitly in some of Hegel's earliest works. In a broadly pantheistic fashion, Hegel conceives of an original unity of "life" (including God, nature, and man). This life loses its "immature" unity as it develops, becoming differentiated into various oppositions: between man and nature, subject and object, master and slave, duty and inclination, divinity and humanity. These oppositions persist as estrangements until life in the one discovers life in the other, through love. The final reconciliation Hegel finds in religion, as man shares in the life of God, as "finite life rises to infinite life." In these early writings of Hegel, one can discern the germs of all of the dimensions of estrangement delineated by Hegel himself, by Feuerbach and Marx, and later by Tillich and Fromm.[4]

In subsequent works, Hegel elaborates a rich concept of estrangement, the primary meaning of which might be termed "self-externalization." He comes to view the development of mind as "the process of becoming an other to itself, i.e., an object for its own self, and in transcending this otherness."[5]

3. It is unnecessary to debate here the relative influence of Hegel and F. W. J. von Schelling (1775–1854) in this area. Since Hegel and Schelling flourished in the same intellectual milieu, it is difficult to determine their relation to each other. Cf. Schelling, *The Ages of the World,* translated with introduction and notes by Frederick de Wolfe Bolman, introduction, pp. 3–79; for Tillich's early analysis of Schelling, cf. Paul Tillich, *Frühe Hauptwerke,* I, pp. 13–108. Both men, in fact, influenced Tillich's thought; but the concept of estrangement had its major development in the Hegelian tradition. It is certainly this tradition which influenced Fromm's view, and we find no substantial reason to question Tillich's statement that Hegel's influence was decisive upon his own thought in this area.

4. Cf. G. W. F. Hegel, "The Spirit of Christianity and its Fate," "Love," and "Fragment of a System," in *On Christianity: Early Theological Writings,* trans. by T. M. Knox.

5. G. W. F. Hegel, *The Phenomenology of Mind,* trans. by J. B. Baillie, Preface, p. 96.

This concept Hegel employs in two significant areas: his philosophy of nature and his philosophy of history. Hegel develops a concept of nature as the externality of the Absolute Mind (or Spirit). Here estrangement becomes a translation of the theological concept of the divine creativity into the metaphysical concept of the divine self-externalization or self-revelation.[6] In his philosophy of history, Hegel formulates a theory of world history as the process through which the universal mind externalizes itself in all of the creations of human culture. It is only as object, outside itself in its creations, that mind can come to know itself.[7] In both of these formulations the universal mind comes to self-consciousness and overcomes its estrangement through the instrumentality of man. Theologically speaking, God comes to awareness of himself through man, as the human mind is elevated to the divine. In these works, Hegel conceives of the reconciliation as taking place through philosophy rather than religion.

Hegel's formulations of the concept of estrangement were criticized in different directions by the young Hegelians. Ludwig Feuerbach (1804–1872) viewed Hegel's work primarily as a speculative effort to clarify and vindicate the traditional Christian theology. Considering it from this point of view, Feuerbach finds in the Hegelian analysis a hidden, as well as an explicit, meaning. The true nature of man's estrangement, according to Feuerbach, is revealed when Hegel's metaphysical theology is discovered to be anthropology. Inverting Hegel's dialectic of estrangement and reconciliation, Feuerbach maintains that man (as "nature," a natural being) projects his own essence into objectivity and views it as God. Estrangement for Feuerbach becomes a movement within man's self-consciousness rather than God's. Philosophical criticism must reveal that Hegel's metaphysic of divine estrangement and reconciliation is really a disguised psychology of human estrangement and reconcilia-

---

6. Cf. Hegel, "The Encyclopaedia of the Philosophical Sciences," excerpted in *Hegel: Selections,* ed. by J. Loewenberg, pp. 176–185.
7. Cf. Hegel, *The Phenomenology of Mind,* pp. 507–610.

tion. In the thought of Feuerbach, God's self-externalization in nature becomes, through inversion, man's projection of his own essence into an imagined objectivity.[8]

Karl Marx (1818–1883) was deeply influenced by Feuerbach's inversion of the Hegelian philosophy. Marx fully accepted Feuerbach's reduction of Hegel's theology to anthropology, but he was not satisfied with Feuerbach's treatment of human estrangement. Marx believed that Feuerbach had accurately reduced man's separation from God to an estrangement within man's own self-consciousness; but Feuerbach had stopped short of an analysis of man's estrangement in "real life," in his productive activities. Feuerbach had dissolved the gods into their human reality; Marx would expose the earthly idols as still more fundamental sources of alienation. For Marx, man's loss of himself in the objects which he creates is the primary alienation; religious estrangement is merely a reflection in consciousness of this alienation in real life. "Religious alienation as such occurs only in the sphere of *consciousness,* in the inner life of man; but economic alienation is that of *real life* and its supersession therefore affects both aspects."[9] For Marx, Feuerbach's failure to detect the most basic form of alienation rendered his analysis abstract and ineffective.

Marx proposed a different kind of revision of the Hegelian dialectic. Feuerbach had inverted Hegel's idealistic philosophy of nature; Marx, however, was primarily interested in Hegel's philosophy of history (especially as it appeared in *The Phenomenology of Mind*). Marx seized upon Hegel's discovery that man actualizes himself in the process of human history through the objective embodiment of his "species-powers" in the creations of human culture. Hegel held that man becomes alienated

8. Cf. Ludwig Feuerbach, *The Essence of Christianity,* trans. by George Eliot, pp. 226–231; this analysis of Feuerbach and subsequently of Marx is indebted to the illuminating exposition in Robert Tucker, *Philosophy and Myth in Karl Marx,* pp. 73–105.

9. Karl Marx, "Economic and Philosophical Manuscripts," in *Marx's Concept of Man,* edited with introduction by Erich Fromm, p. 128.

from these powers in the process of objectifying them. Man gives embodiment to his own nature in cultural creativity, and in so doing he becomes estranged from this nature.

Marx accepted this analysis of man's self-production, but he held that Hegel formulated the idea only in an abstract way. According to Marx, Hegel started with abstract mind or self-consciousness. The creations of mind were then viewed as thought products, states of consciousness. Alienation for Hegel, therefore, consisted only of a movement within self-consciousness, not a movement in real life.

For Hegel, *human life, man,* is equivalent to *self-consciousness.* All alienation of human life is therefore nothing but *alienation of* self-consciousness. The alienation of self-consciousness is not regarded as the *expression,* reflected in knowledge and thought, of the *real* alienation of human life.[10]

Marx's criticisms of Hegel and Feuerbach are essentially the same: both view estrangement abstractly as a movement within consciousness rather than concretely as a movement which has an objective reality. Marx accepts Feuerbach's inversion of the Hegelian theology. But inversion of the dialectical movement is not enough; it must be made to apply to "real corporeal *man,* with his feet firmly planted on the solid ground."

In Marx's account, then, man as a natural being "produces" his own nature or species-powers in history through actual labor, embodying these powers in material goods and in instruments of material production, as well as in social institutions and systems of ideas. In all products of his creativity, man objectifies himself; and in so doing he loses himself in estrangement. Alienation occurs in all production, but especially in material production, since man is first of all a material being. In Marx's view, then, the Hegelian metaphysics is an "esoteric economics" rather than as with Feuerbach, an "esoteric psychology."[11]

Marx's concept of productivity requires further explanation.

10. *Ibid.,* p. 179.
11. Tucker, *Philosophy and Myth in Karl Marx,* p. 120.

In a sense, for Marx, man creates the world in which he lives; he "produces" nature itself. This theme can be viewed as another aspect of the transformation of theology into anthropology. Man, not God, is the creator. But man's relation to nature is creation only in a modified sense, a kind of reproduction. There is an original objectivity of nature which is presupposed, a precondition for creativity. It is not this sheer objectivity of nature which constitutes alienation for Marx. Rather, the external world becomes alien to man when man's own productive activity with regard to the world is alienated activity. Estrangement is first a quality of man's activity, and only thereafter is it a quality of the world which he creates.

What, then, is alienated activity according to Marx? It is the state of affairs wherein a man's labor is no longer within his own control. And since a man's productive powers can be taken from his control only by another man, Marx sees the source of alienated activity in "the division of labor" and "private property"—that is, in the control of one man's labor and of the products of his labor by another man. Thus the ultimate source of alienation in the Marxian analysis is the division between man and man (a division within the species "man"), appearing when one man produces and another controls his production.

> Every self-alienation of man, from himself and from nature, appears in the relation which he postulates between other men and himself and nature. Thus religious self-alienation is necessarily exemplified in the relation between laity and priest, or, since it is here a question of the spiritual world, between the laity and a mediator. In the real world of practice this self-alienation can only be expressed in the real, practical relation of man to his fellowmen. The medium through which alienation occurs is itself a *practical* one.[12]

In summary, we have uncovered three distinct, though related, meanings of estrangement in the Hegelian tradition. (1) Hegel's original conception was primarily metaphysical. He

12. Marx, "Economic and Philosophical Manuscripts," in *Marx's Concept of Man*, p. 105.

suggested that various forms of self-externalization are necessary for the full actualization of being. In his earliest writings, the self-separating reality is conceptualized as "life," a concept which can be interpreted in a naturalistic-pantheistic fashion. Later, Hegel conceives of self-consciousness as the self-separating entity; estrangement is then conceived in idealistic terms as a movement within the Divine Mind. (2) Feuerbach reduced this metaphysical movement to a psychological phenomenon which can be described as "projection." In this interpretation of estrangement, man attributes his own essential qualities to an imagined external being; as a result, at least in his own self-consciousness, man does not see these qualities as inherent in his own nature. (3) Marx viewed both of these analyses of estrangement as abstract versions of the real phenomenon of alienation. For him, estrangement in the real world is that form of human activity in which spontaneous creativity is transformed into forced labor, so that self-production becomes self-loss. This occurs when one man controls the labor of another. Alienation in consciousness is a reflection of this alienation in "real life." We shall encounter all three meanings of estrangement in our study of Tillich and Fromm. Distinctive features of the three approaches should be kept in mind. Since they are sometimes woven together in an unclear manner, it will serve the end of clarity to be able to distinguish them.

In spite of these important distinctions, it is possible to identify essential features in all ideas of estrangement. If the following statement by Heinemann were extended to include the Divine Being as well as human beings, it might serve as a comprehensive description of these essential features:

> The facts to which the term "alienation" refers, are, objectively, different kinds of dissociation, break or rupture between human beings and their objects, whether the latter be other persons, or the natural world, or their own creations in art, science and society; and subjectively, the corresponding states of disequilibrium, disturbance, strangeness and anxiety. . . . There is one point common to

all of them, i.e. the belief that a preceding unity and harmony has been transformed into disunity and disharmony.[13]

Existentialism, Estrangement, and the Method of Correlation

We are now in a position to examine Tillich's theological method in greater detail. We have noted that Tillich seeks to take seriously the nontheological analysis of man produced by modern culture. This means that in Tillich's view the analysis of the human predicament is a task for philosophy rather than theology, and that in this task the philosopher must draw upon interpretive materials from all realms of culture—art, literature, drama, etc.—as well as upon philosophical insight per se. This seemingly inexhaustible body of material concerning man is narrowed down, however, by the viewpoint which Tillich adopts toward it. According to Tillich, when man analyzes his own existence he inevitably deals with "existential" terms and categories. This type of analysis is to be found in all eras and cannot be exclusively identified with any one school of philosophy. In Tillich's view, however, it is especially characteristic of the contemporary movement known as existentialism. Tillich considers the literature of this movement (interpreted broadly to include psychoanalysis and "depth sociology") to be the most significant analysis of the human predicament to emerge in the modern period.[14] Therefore, it is primarily this literature with which Christian theology must enter into dialogue.

Briefly stated, Tillich understands the main effort of existentialism to be "an analysis of what it means to exist."[15] Human existence itself proves to be the problem which man must face —the question which demands an answer. This seemingly innocent definition leads Tillich to an important conclusion about existentialist analysis. Human existence not only *raises* certain perennial questions; it *is* itself the question which underlies all

13. Heinemann, *Existentialism and the Modern Predicament*, p. 9.
14. Cf. Tillich, *Systematic Theology*, II, pp. 26–28. In his discussions of existentialism, Tillich mentions Schelling, Feuerbach, Kierkegaard, Marx, Nietzsche, Heidegger, and Sartre, among others.
15. *Ibid.,* p. 25.

others. If this is the case, then analysis of human existence is analysis of the *problem*, of the *question*. And one does not expect to derive an answer from an analysis of the question; answers are addressed to the question, not derived from it. Therefore, Tillich holds in principle that existentialism develops the question implied in human existence but cannot as such provide answers to it. Answers have many sources, but they do not come from existentialist analysis.

This methodological definition of existentialism is of limited value until it is combined with the specific content which Tillich finds in all existentialist analysis. This content is the understanding of existence as estrangement. To explain this aspect of existentialism, Tillich traces the origin of the movement to certain nineteenth-century protests against the Hegelian philosophy. The existentialists, according to Tillich, accepted Hegel's concept of estranged existence but rejected as premature and ineffective his efforts at reconciliation through thought.

The common point in all existentialist attacks is that man's existential situation is a state of estrangement from his essential nature. Hegel is aware of this estrangement, but he believes that it has been overcome and that man has been reconciled with his true being. According to all the existentialists, this belief is Hegel's basic error. Reconciliation is a matter of anticipation and expectation, but not of reality. . . . Existence is estrangement and not reconciliation.[16]

It is this understanding of existence as estrangement which explains Tillich's argument that for the existentialists existence itself is the human problem. His position is that the analysis of existence leads inevitably to the discovery of estrangement.

As the passage quoted above indicates, Tillich speaks of estrangement as the separation of a being from its "essential nature," as an alienation of existence from "essence." This terminology, reminiscent of Plato as well as Hegel, introduces new issues not immediately suggested by the term estrangement. By incorporating this distinction into the idea of estrangement, Tillich invests the concept with epistemological as well as

16. *Ibid.*

axiological and ontological dimensions. It might be observed here that although many existentialists do deal in some way with the problem of estrangement, it is not at all apparent that they are agreed in understanding it as "the separation of essence and existence." Sartre, for example, is usually interpreted as having rejected the idea that man has a fixed nature.[17] In a later section we shall develop Tillich's answer to this criticism: his argument that the concept of estrangement necessarily involves the distinction of essence and existence and that Sartre and others make surreptitious use of the distinction while denying its validity. Our reconsideration of Tillich's method in the next section will seek to clarify his position further by introducing the category of self-estrangement as another way of expressing his viewpoint.

We may now draw together the threads of our discussion up to this point. Tillich's theological method seeks to correlate the "answers" of the Christian message with the "questions" posed by man's contemporary self-analysis. This analysis is necessarily existentialist; it examines human existence itself. The consensus of existentialist insight, according to Tillich's summation, is that existence is characterized by estrangement. This multidimensional category is identified in all dimensions as the separation of that which ought to be united. In Tillich's formulation of the existentialist insight, this means the separation of existence from essence, of the estranged being from its own essential nature. This, according to Tillich, is the basic problem of man with which Christian doctrine must be correlated.

17. Cf. I. M. Bochenski, *Contemporary European Philosophy*, pp. 177–178.

II

the method
Reconsidered

Criticism and a Proposal TILLICH'S approach
to the ideas of estrangement which he finds in existentialist literature involves an important assumption which must now be
examined.[1] Tillich assumes that estrangement must mean total
estrangement—total in the sense that every aspect of man's existence is affected by this condition. This is implicit in his contention that human existence is itself the question and that no
answers can be derived from existential analysis. It is also implicit in his understanding of estrangement as the separation of
essence and existence.

To take a specific example, Tillich at one point notes that
some analysts view estrangement in modern society as the result
of "the structures of industrial society," an understanding which
leads them to hold that estrangement can be eliminated through
a change in those structures. Tillich argues that it is a fallacious
utopianism which holds "the belief that changes in the structure
of our society would, as such, change man's existential predicament."[2] The point is that if estrangement is recognized only
in some special area of human life (e.g., a particular social
structure), then it can be eliminated by man through a reform
of that area. This would mean that estrangement is no longer

1. With reference to the material in this chapter, cf. my article,
"An Examination of Tillich's Method of Correlation," *The Journal of
Bible and Religion*, XXXII (July 1964) pp. 248–251.
2. Tillich, *Systematic Theology*, II, p. 74.

viewed as a characteristic of human existence as such, a position which Tillich rejects.[3]

Tillich does not, in fact, find agreement among the existentialists that estrangement is total in this sense. As he admits, some apply ideas of estrangement to special areas of life. Practically all seek to provide answers to the human predicament either explicitly or implicitly. Tillich's recognition of this leads him to the position that when existentialists give "answers" they do so, not as existentialists, but as participants in some religious or quasi-religious tradition. Existentialism must remain philosophical analysis of "the question implied in existence"; all answers are religious.[4] Thus defining existentialism, in effect, as analysis of *estranged existence*, Tillich considers all other aspects of the writings of this group to be nonexistentialist.

It might be questioned whether this approach to existentialism is entirely adequate. Two criticisms of it might be suggested. First, this formulation overlooks the point that question and answer are interrelated. If estrangement is viewed as merely partial, then some answer can be derived from the human situation, from the unalienated aspect. Only if estrangement is viewed as total can it be said that no answer can be derived from the human situation. But the existentialists do not, in fact, agree upon the extent of estrangement. Tillich seems to employ an implicit definition of existentialism which the existentialists themselves do not accept. Thus he brings to bear a critique of the ideas of estrangement, rather than accepting these ideas as autonomous philosophical analysis and simply organizing them for theological purposes.

Second, this formulation of the method allows Tillich to ignore the "answers" of the existentialists to the problem of estrangement. This methodological disregard for the philosophical answers leaves the theologian subject to the charge of

3. The fact that Tillich uses "existence" in a restricted technical sense will concern us later in the study.
4. Tillich, *Systematic Theology,* II, p. 25.

"heteronomy" or authoritarianism when he seeks to correlate the theological answers with the existential questions.

These criticisms of Tillich's approach to existentialism can be dealt with through a refinement in our understanding of the method of correlation. This modification is suggested by certain comments of Tillich himself concerning the religious nature of ideas of estrangement and reconciliation. In an important essay on the subject, Tillich suggests that these concepts presuppose certain Christian doctrines. "The modern ideas of estrangement and reconciliation . . . must be considered as autonomous developments of fundamental Christian principles."[5] Later, Tillich again suggests that these ideas have a religious basis. "Actually, even the awareness of estrangement and the desire for salvation are effects of the presence of saving power, in other words, revelatory experiences."[6]

According to this approach, existentialist analyses, or ideas of estrangement and reconciliation, are based either upon a fragmentary universal revelation, or, more concretely, upon the Christian tradition. This is apparently what Tillich means when he suggests viewing them as "self-estranged theology." This does not mean that theology can accept the autonomous development of either idea as a substitute for Christian theology. They are incomplete; they must both be "elevated beyond themselves."

Yet . . . Christian theology should not surrender to modern thought. . . . She should reconcile them by elevating them at the same time beyond themselves as *agape* does, and as great apologetic theology has always done. There are questions left in each of the ideas of estrangement and reconciliation, questions for which the Christian message is the ultimate answer.[7]

5. Paul Tillich, "Estrangement and Reconciliation in Modern Thought," *Review of Religion,* IX (November, 1944), p. 19.

6. Tillich, *Systematic Theology,* II, p. 86. This religious element is to be distinguished from the awareness of being-itself which Tillich sees as the basis of all philosophy. Ontology assumes, and seeks, being-itself; but existentialism assumes, and seeks, the "New Being."

7. Tillich, "Estrangement and Reconciliation in Modern Thought," p. 19.

These statements suggest a modified interpretation of existentialism and of the method of correlation. Here, not just the "question," but both question and answer are existentialist; at the same time, not just the answers, but both question and answer are religious. Since there is no sharp distinction between question and answer, both are of interest to theology. On the other hand, neither the formulation of the question (estrangement) nor the answer (reconciliation) can be accepted without criticism by Christian theology; for question and answer are interdependent. If, for example, reconciling power is derived from some aspect of human existence, this implies that estrangement is only partial. Nontheological ideas of estrangement and reconciliation must be "elevated beyond themselves" through theological criticism.

This interpretation of existentialism, viewing it as an autonomous development of certain religious principles, removes the methodological difficulties cited above. It is now unnecessary to interpret existentialism in abstraction from the ever-present ideas of reconciliation. At the same time, it would seem to render the theological answers less heteronomous, since they are viewed as an "elevation" of the autonomous answers rather than being unrelated to them. The theological critique of ideas of estrangement is now explicit rather than surreptitious. What is being claimed, then, is that the understanding of man which sees the human condition as, in some sense, an estrangement is essentially a religious intuition (in contrast, for example, to philosophies which see no human predicament as such). Existentialism, that is, may be viewed by Christian theology as a kind of "natural anthropology" (rather than a natural theology).

The Criterion of Self-estrangement

We must now examine more closely the idea of elevating autonomous ideas of estrangement and reconciliation beyond themselves. To achieve this, some criterion is required which would drive the philosophical formulation of the question of man to the point where no autonomous answer is possible. This theological critique, at the same time, should not violate the data of the existentialist analysis. It would appear that Tillich finds such a criterion in his concept of "self-estrangement."

As we have shown, the concept of estrangement in all of its forms implies that some original unity or harmony has been re-placed by disunity or disharmony. This original unity may be conceived, especially in a philosophy which tends toward monism, as an original identity of some sort. It is this version which characterizes the Hegelian tradition. In his early writings, commenting upon the Bible verse, "God is spirit, and they that worship him must worship him in spirit and in truth," John 4:24, Hegel states:

How could anything but a spirit know a spirit? The relation of spirit to spirit is a feeling of harmony, is their unification; how could heterogeneity be unified? Faith in the divine is only possible if in the believer himself there is a divine element which rediscovers itself, its own nature, in that on which it believes, even if it be un-conscious that what it has found *is* its own nature. . . . Hence faith in the divine grows out of the divinity of the believer's own nature; only a modification of the Godhead can know the Godhead.[8]

This understanding of estrangement as separation from an original identity underlies the entire Hegelian perspective. At the same time, it becomes the basis for the Feuerbachian inver-sion. If Hegel has man finding himself in God, Feuerbach has man finding God in himself. Marx accepts Feuerbach's critique but has man finding himself in his other creations as well.

In a well-known essay, Tillich essentially reproduces the Hegelian understanding of man's separation from and reunion with God. In the philosophy of religion which he espouses, "man discovers himself when he discovers God; he discovers something that is identical with himself although it transcends

8. Hegel, "The Spirit of Christianity and its Fate," in *On Christianity: Early Theological Writings,* p. 266.

him infinitely, something from which he is estranged, but from which he never has been and never can be separated."[9] This is what is meant in Tillich's usage by the term *self-estrangement:* man is separated from his own true being. This concept provides the basis for Tillich's idea of "theonomy," where God's law is viewed as the law of man's own life; and it illuminates his conception of religion as "ultimate concern": man can only be "totally concerned about the totality which is his true being."[10]

Although Tillich does not always preserve the distinction in his usage, the term self-estrangement takes on a specific meaning in his system in relation to other possible types of estrangement. Tillich uses the term to indicate the seriousness, the completeness, of the estrangement. If man is self-estranged, every aspect of his total existence needs healing or reconciliation. He is not separated from a part of himself but from the totality of his nature. This signification of the term is indicated by Tillich in the following passage:

> Estrangement, in contrast to reconciliation, describes the disruption of an essential unity and consequently a destructive situation. The estrangement of casual friends from each other or of a man from a casual interest has no catastrophical character. But if subject and object of the estrangement are identical, an intolerable situation arises; estrangement then becomes self-alienation, the threat of losing oneself and the pain of contradicting oneself result from such an immanent estrangement, and a quest for reconciliation is the necessary consequence of it.[11]

The conception of an estrangement where "subject and object of the estrangement are identical" raises questions which will be dealt with throughout this study. Our contention here is that Tillich's method of correlation is built around the idea of existence as self-estrangement.

The use of the word "self" here may be ambiguous. We have

9. Tillich, "The Two Types of Philosophy of Religion," in *Theology of Culture,* ed. by Robert C. Kimball, p. 10. As we shall see, Fromm essentially reproduces the position of Feuerbach and Marx.

10. Tillich, *Systematic Theology,* I, p. 14.

11. Tillich, "Estrangement and Reconciliation in Modern Thought," p. 6.

been referring largely to the estrangement of human beings, or "selves," but for Tillich the term "self-estrangement" has a broader application.

Self-estrangement can arise within a we-self as well as within an ego-self; it can occur within the unity of life as a whole, and in the unity of the divine ground of life; it can occur in the community of the knowing and the known, as well as of the loving and the loved. In each of these cases self-estrangement is the absolute threat and reconciliation the absolute demand, for a living unity.[12]

In any of these cases of self-estrangement the being is estranged from its own identity, its own nature. In its existence it has become separated from its essence. It is totally, not partially, estranged.

This then is the theological criterion which Tillich implicitly applies to existentialist ideas of estrangement—they are pushed or "elevated" to the point of self-estrangement. The method of correlation assumes that man's existence in its totality is a question, a predicament. If man as a totality is separated from something to which he belongs, this can be no *part* of himself which is lost but his whole self; he is self-estranged. Where existentialist ideas do not go this far, they must be criticized and elevated to the point of self-estrangement. But when this point is reached no autonomous answer is possible; an answer from beyond estranged existence, and therefore a theological answer, is required. What we are suggesting is an interpretation of Tillich's method which views it, not as a correlation between philosophical questions and theological answers, but as an "elevation" through the criterion of self-estrangement of inherently religious ideas of estrangement and reconciliation into the framework of Christian theology.

The Problem Restated

Following this understanding of the method, our effort to relate Fromm's analysis of human existence to Tillich's theological system, then, will take the form of an experiment in elevation.

12. *Ibid.*

First, Fromm's ideas of alienation and reconciliation will be examined in the context of his general perspective. After an introduction to Tillich's systematic structure from the point of view suggested here, we shall then consider what would be involved in "elevating" a concept of estrangement such as Fromm's to the point of self-estrangement, where no autonomous answer is possible. This investigation will serve two purposes: it will enable us to determine what kind of critique Tillich might bring to bear upon Fromm's perspective, and we shall be in a position to consider what bearing Tillich's criterion of self-estrangement has upon his account of the Christian answers to the problem of estrangement. This will involve an examination of the meaning of divine self-estrangement, the terminal concept in Tillich's system. It is thus hoped that an effective comparison of naturalistic and theistic ideas of estrangement will be achieved. To this dialogue we now turn.

III

ERICH
FROMM
AND HIS MENTORS

ERICH FROMM was
born in Frankfurt, Germany, in 1900. He received his education at the Universities of Heidelberg and Munich and his
specialized training at the Berlin Psychoanalytic Institute and
the Institute for Social Research of the University of Frankfurt.
He also lectured at the two latter institutions. With the rise to
power of Hitler in 1932, Fromm came to the United States,
where he taught at several colleges. At present he is Professor
of Psychology at New York University and Professor of Psychoanalysis at the National University of Mexico in Mexico City.[1]

Fromm's thought is best understood initially as an effort to
reconcile and synthesize the insights of Freudian psychoanalysis
and Marxian sociology. This judgment, suggested by a close
reading of Fromm's major works, is confirmed in his auto-
biographical essay, *Beyond the Chains of Illusion: My Encounter
with Marx and Freud.* We shall begin, then, by showing how
Fromm comes to terms with each of his mentors.

Fromm and Freud

Fromm is frequently identified as a psychoanalyst. The his-
torians of psychoanalysis, however, distinguish his views from
those of contemporary Freudians. Fromm is usually classified

1. For other biographical data, cf. Erich Fromm, *Beyond the Chains
of Illusion,* pp. 3–12.

as a "Neo-Freudian" or a "Neo-Freudian revisionist." Herbert
Marcuse, for example, places Fromm at the center of the spec-
trum of "Neo-Freudian revisionism." [2]

The revision of Freud undertaken by Fromm (along with
others similarly classified, such as Karen Horney and Harry
Stack Sullivan) is generally understood to be the attempt to
show the relevance of social structures and relations to the psychoanalytic concepts. Karen Horney identifies Fromm as the
first writer in German psychoanalytic literature to recognize the
importance of cultural factors. Clara Thompson indicates that
Fromm "retains a broad social perspective in studying psychological phenomena," and that he sees the role of society "in
creating man as well as controlling him." [3] On the basis of this
emphasis, Marcuse places Fromm in a "cultural and inter-
personal school" of psychoanalysis.

This classification of Fromm as a "Neo-Freudian revisionist"
is challenged, however, in a recent full-length study of Fromm's
work. In his useful analysis, J. H. Schaar suggests that this
classification of Fromm is misleading. With some exaggeration,
he argues that Fromm's attitude toward Freud's work is that of
opposition, not reform.

It is certainly true that Fromm has carried on a one-sided argument
with Freud for something over a quarter of a century, but an argument which embraces values Freud shunned, starts from premises
he rejected, accepts types of evidence unknown to him, employs
methods he denied, and leads to different conclusions on all the
basic issues ought to be called what it is—opposition and not revision, revolt and not reform. Fromm is a revisionist of Freud in
about the same degree, if not in the same direction, that the Prince
of Darkness was a revisionist of the Prince of Light. [4]

In my opinion, Schaar's description of Fromm's opposition to

2. Herbert Marcuse, *Eros and Civilization*, p. 238.
3. Clara Thompson, *Psychoanalysis: Its Evolution and Development*,
p. 143.
4. John H. Schaar, *Escape from Authority*, pp. 7–8. In his recent
work, *The Heart of Man*, Fromm himself rejects the label of "neo-
Freudian."

Freud, though overdrawn, does point correctly to a wide divergence between the thought of the two men. It is possible, however, to gain insight into the genesis and development of Fromm's thought by viewing it as a revision of the Freudian perspective. We shall, therefore, first approach Fromm in these terms, seeking to determine how far and in which directions he is carried in his revisions of Freud. When this has been done it will be clear that another major influence—that of Marx—must be acknowledged. We shall show that, although developmentally it is legitimate to view Fromm as a Freudian revisionist, any classification of his mature thought ought also to include reference to his Marxian roots.

The origins of Fromm's methodology can be found in his efforts to relate social psychology to psychoanalysis. In an early essay, Fromm suggests that the method of a "psychoanalytic social psychology" can, in most respects, be the same as that of psychoanalysis. It cannot take the social group as its object; rather, its proper concern is with the psychic attitudes of individuals—that is, those attitudes common to most individuals in a given society. It can be presumed that these common attitudes derive from common experiences rooted in the society's life patterns. Just as psychoanalysis studies the effect of childhood experiences upon the individual's psychic attitudes, so social psychology investigates "how certain psychic attitudes common to members of a group are related to their common life experiences."[5]

How, then, are these common attitudes, derived from the prevailing life patterns of the society, incorporated into the individual character structure? According to psychoanalytic theory, the matrix of character is in early childhood, the period of least direct influence from the larger society. Does the society then play no dynamic and formative role in individual character development?

To show that society does play a significant role in character

5. Erich Fromm, "The Dogma of Christ," in Fromm, *The Dogma of Christ and Other Essays on Religion, Psychology and Culture*, p. 9.

formation, Fromm in this same essay speaks of a "repetition" in the adult of the "psychic situation of childhood." Because of this repetition, psychic dependence is maintained through the same "mechanisms" which make the child psychically dependent upon his father. Here Fromm reflects the Freudian view that man's relation to socially maintained authority figures represents a "transference" from the paternal relationship. In Freud's expression, "that which began in relation to the father ends in relation to the community." [6] For Freud, the familial relationships are irreducible and primal; the society's influence in shaping individual character is derivative and secondary.

The theory of repetition, however, leads to a dilemma. According to this theory, the individual must achieve a degree of maturity before becoming exposed to the psychic demands of the society. Fromm observes that the psychically immature person remains fixated in the situation of childhood; it is the normal person whose psychic attitudes are determined to a significant degree by "the socially conditioned life pattern." [7] This means that only those individuals who have overcome infantile dependencies are subject to a repetition of these dependencies in relation to socially defined structures of authority. The process of growth toward maturity in this account becomes self-defeating.

Fromm's subsequent thought can be understood largely as an effort to describe (more successfully) the role of society in individual character formation. Fromm seeks to achieve this goal by developing two fundamental revisions of the Freudian perspective.

First, Fromm comes to reject Freud's view that certain familial relationships are universal and independent of the social structure. Fromm reverses this position in his thesis that the family is "the psychic agency of society." [8] This means that for

6. Sigmund Freud, *Civilization and its Discontents*, p. 89.
7. Fromm, "The Dogma of Christ," in *The Dogma of Christ and Other Essays*, p. 9.
8. Fromm, *The Sane Society*, p. 82. Fromm was influenced at this point, no doubt, by the early writings of Karl Marx.

Fromm the particular configuration of the familial relationships is largely derived from the general life pattern of a particular society. The family in a certain society tends to produce in its offspring a character structure desired or approved by that society. The society exerts a formative influence upon the child through parental influence.

This understanding of character formation is the basis for Fromm's concept of the "social character," that "nucleus of the character structure which is shared by most members of the same culture." [9] This formulation recognizes that there are important individual character differences within a given culture; individual psychoanalysis is concerned with these. But Fromm maintains that the shared life patterns of a given culture produce a common core of character traits in its individual members, and it is this "social character" which is the proper concern of a psychoanalytic social psychology. This approach to social influence upon character formation avoids the difficulties connected with the theory of repetition described above. Here, the influence of the society through the agency of the family is a primary factor in forming individual character.

This revised approach to character formation has far-reaching consequences which will concern us throughout our study of Fromm. When the role of the society in character formation is emphasized, the attention of the social psychologist is turned from individual pathology to social pathology, or, more specifically, to the "socially patterned defect" in individual character structure. Fromm's work in contrast to Freud's is therefore characterized by a prevailing interest in social pathology and in the possibility of social health or "the sane society." [10] Concepts which originated in the area of individual pathology now take on new meanings, and new concepts emerge which, in turn, require changes in individual psychoanalysis.

9. *Ibid.*, p. 78.
10. Cf. *ibid.*, pp. 12–21. Fromm has Freud's warrant for this investigation, although Freud himself did not undertake it. Cf. Freud, *Civilization and its Discontents*, p. 104.

In considering society's role in shaping human character, Fromm does, in fact, arrive at a significant re-estimate of individual desires and passions—an approach which suggests a major change in psychoanalytic theory. Here we find a second fundamental revision of the Freudian perspective.

Freud consistently understood the multifarious desires and passions of men to be rooted in physiological sources. This is true, not only in Freud's analysis of libido development, but also in his treatment of ego maturation and the process of socialization. Freud traced the evolution of the sexual instinct through several stages of libidinal satisfaction (the oral, anal, and genital levels of libido fixation); he saw the development of the ego as a means of taking account of external reality, so that the individual may preserve himself and secure the greatest libidinal satisfaction possible.[11]

The process of socialization was understood by Freud largely as a process of restraining, redirecting, and sublimating the physiological desires. The super-ego, which emerges as the product of parental authority, derives its power from the redirection of aggressive instincts toward the self. The aims of human culture and civilization can be achieved only through a sublimation of the libidinal instincts. Freud postulated that the demands of civilization function as a "cultural super-ego" in the lives of individuals.[12] Civilization for Freud thus rests precariously upon the basis of the redirected and sublimated physiological drives. In short, all of the various passions of men have a physiological root.

Fromm's analysis of the fundamental human desires and passions is not a denial of the factors which Freud identified; it is rather a major shift in emphasis which sharply reduces their significance. Fromm does not reject Freud's analysis of the evolution of the sexual instinct in the maturing individual; but

11. Cf. Freud, *A General Introduction to Psychoanalysis*, pp. 287–312.
12. Cf. Freud, *Civilization and its Discontents*, pp. 94–103.

he sees a far more important evolution which overshadows the physiological process: the evolution of consciousness. Freud acknowledged that the ego must go through developmental stages parallel to, but partially independent of, the libido development, although this process was not his main interest; but he retained the notion that this process could be analyzed in terms of physiological motivations. Fromm, however, maintains that the appearance of human self-awareness creates imperative new needs which have no physiological root. The quest for a satisfaction of these distinctively human needs initiates a new process of development, built upon the physical body but transcending it. It is at this point that Fromm makes his most radical departure from the Freudian perspective.

Fromm maintains that the distinctive characteristics of human existence appear when, in the course of biological evolution, man becomes aware of himself as a separate individual. This awareness leads to a sense of aloneness and to a compelling need to achieve "a new relatedness to man and nature after having lost the primary relatedness of the pre-human stage."[13] This sense of aloneness constitutes the universal human predicament, although the ways in which the need is defined and the ways in which it is met are diverse. The drive for a new relatedness supplants the physiological drives as man's most intensive and dominant passion.

We observed earlier that it was Fromm's consideration of society's role in shaping human character which led him to re-estimate human needs and passions; we now see clearly his thesis that it is society's role in shaping the content of human consciousness which has a profound effect upon human character. Fromm holds the view, derived as we shall see from Marx, that consciousness is itself a social product. Through various means (discussed below), society determines to a large extent what is included in, and excluded from, consciousness. Fromm's

13. Fromm, *The Sane Society,* p. viii.

interest, then, is in the evolutionary development of consciousness (in the individual and in all humanity) and in society's role in fostering or retarding that development.

In tracing the development of consciousness, Fromm seeks to delineate identifiable stages in the process and its final goal. It is here that Fromm's work most clearly displays its composite character; for Fromm has sought to analyze this process in both Freudian and Marxian terms. The Marxian aspect will be analyzed in the next section.

As to the stages in the evolution of individual consciousness, or what he calls "orientations" toward reality, Fromm undertakes a "symbolic" interpretation of Freud's stages of libido development. Freud identified certain observable character types as representing progressive fixations of the energy of the sexual drive. He saw the normally developing individual evolving toward the primacy of the genital zone in achieving sexual satisfaction. Fromm does not deny that this physiological evolution takes place. However, he interprets the character types identified by Freud as types of relatedness, as ways in which *psychic* energy is "channelized." Thus they become types of "social character" which have no physiological root. The goal of the normally evolving individual is the "productive orientation," the type of character which is creative psychically as well as physically.[14]

This transformation of the Freudian categories turns our attention to the society which fosters or inhibits the development of productive individuals. A healthy society will tend to produce a healthy social character in its individuals. Fromm, following a suggestion made by Freud, postulates that there is an "obvious analogy between the evolution of the human race, and the evolution of the individual."[15] Thus one may speak of human history in terms of an evolution from infancy to maturity. This means that a primitive society would tend to produce certain

14. For Fromm's description of Freud's categories and his transformation of them, cf. Fromm, *Man for Himself*, pp. 35–37; 82–107.
15. Fromm, *The Sane Society*, p. 70.

infantile fixations (not necessarily physiological ones), while a mature society would tend to produce productive character types. The history of man is the story of his evolution toward maturity.

This effort to analyze human history in terms of a process toward maturity stands twice removed from Freud's description of libido development. The physiological categories were transformed into psychic concepts, then taken from man's individual growth and applied to his historical development. Further, Fromm does not seem to hold that the stages which Freud delineated (and which he interprets symbolically) fit the evolution of mankind in progressive sequence. For example, he finds two nonproductive character types combining in the twentieth-century social character of the West; and these in no sense represent a progressive development from the two equally nonproductive types which he finds in the nineteenth-century Western society.[16] Indeed, one major form of the twentieth-century character type (the "marketing orientation") has no relation, even symbolically, to the Freudian categories.

We must conclude that the two fundamental revisions of Freud surveyed here represent a major reformulation of the entire psychoanalytic perspective. Fromm's developmental history of human relatedness cannot be viewed as Neo-Freudian revisionism if this means simply the extension of Freudian principles into virgin territory. Rather, Fromm's wide-ranging considerations carry him beyond the gravitational field of any Freudian school and into a new orbit—that of German idealism and the inversion of idealism in Feuerbach and Marx.

Fromm and Marx

Fromm's configuration of ideas concerning the social influence on the content of consciousness was decisively influenced

16. *Ibid.*, p. 136. In *The Heart of Man*, Fromm argues that neither Freud's libido fixations nor his own character orientations can be arranged in evolutionary order. Rather, within each category there can be a greater or lesser degree of pathology or regression. Cf. pp. 111–113.

by Marx's early philosophical writings. Marx postulated that the content of human consciousness is largely determined by the structure of his social existence; this structure is in turn determined by the "mode of production in material life."[17] In other words, Marx held that man's conscious ideas in the areas of law, politics, philosophy, and religion (what Marx called "ideology") are to be understood "scientifically" in terms of their material basis in the "economic conditions of production." A change in the latter leads to a corresponding change in the former. Thus, for Marx, the history of man's conscious thought about himself and his world is determined in its general development by the evolution of the modes of material production and the control of production. This evolution, not the development of man's thought about himself, is the truly significant process.

In his interpretation of Marxian thought, Fromm attempts to correct what he takes to be a common misapprehension concerning Marx's "historical materialism." He argues that Marxism, contrary to the popular notion, is not a theory concerned primarily with the nature of human needs and motivations. It does not hold, for example, that the desire for material gain is the primary human motive. Rather, the theory is concerned with the "objectively given conditions" which give shape and direction to human desires. These conditions determine the mode of production; hence they determine man's understanding of his own needs. These conditions can determine man's conscious thought because his needs and drives (beyond certain fixed needs) are themselves socially produced and indefinitely flexible.[18]

In Fromm's account, Marx's materialism is not a psychological theory—the reduction of all human motives to a physical basis. It is rather a sociological theory—the explanation of man's cultural development and thought in terms of his total mode of life. This means to Fromm that Marx reached a uni-

17. Karl Marx, "Excerpt from *A Contribution to the Critique of Political Economy*," in *Marx and Engels*, ed. Lewis S. Feuer, p. 43.
18. Erich Fromm, *Marx's Concept of Man*, pp. 12–14.

fied view of man which understands his consciousness as rooted in the conditions of his existence.

Marx, in his dialectic method, overcame the materialism of the nineteenth century and developed a truly dynamic and holistic theory based on man's *activity*, rather than on his *physiology*.[19]

Fromm admits, however, that the Marxian economic determinism is one-sided. Marx saw clearly man's "false consciousness"—the irrational self-understanding, the perverted needs and drives of men—but he held that these are caused solely by economic conditions. Therefore, he thought that man could be changed easily through a change in the objective economic situation. According to Fromm, Marx underestimated the force of the nonphysical needs of man which stem from the very conditions of human existence (which include self-awareness). These needs are served by the cultural and ideological factors. Without the development of a more productive satisfaction of these needs, a change in the economic conditions will, in Fromm's view, remain an inadequate solution to man's basic problems. History must be understood as the interaction of economic conditions and the fundamental needs of human nature which transcend the purely physical.[20]

We find then that Fromm suggests a revision of Marx not unlike his revision of Freud. If (contra Freud) it is not the physiological libido which is responsible for the primary human passions, neither is it (contra Marx) the economic necessities which are the fundamental driving forces of human activity. Both types of physiological need are important, but they must be viewed in interaction with the distinctively human needs arising from self-consciousness. And it is clear that Fromm finally subordinates the former to the latter. Fromm holds that Marx is not blind to either type of need, although he tends to subordinate the nonphysical to the physical.

19. Fromm, *The Sane Society,* p. 262. This means in modern terminology that Fromm interprets Marx as an existentialist.
20. Cf. *ibid.,* pp. 261–265.

Marx's analysis of false consciousness centered in the concept of alienation which he inherited from Hegel and Feuerbach, as we have seen. In *The German Ideology,* Marx sought to show how alienation appeared in man's social evolution through the advent of the division of labor and private property. When he lost control over his own creative activity he became alienated from himself, his fellow man, and nature. This alienation will be overcome in man's historical development, according to Marx, when class divisions are eliminated and society as a whole controls production. In this society, the split within humanity (both in the individual and the society) will be overcome.[21]

Fromm's criticism of Marx's economic determinism can be applied in a similar fashion to his concept of alienation. Fromm argues that Marx is unduly optimistic in holding that man can be changed by a change in the external situation. According to Fromm, the structure of man's awareness of himself and his world is deeply affected by the state of alienation and is not easily changed.

The famous statement at the end of the Communist Manifesto that the workers "have nothing to lose but their chains," contains a profound psychological error. With their chains they have to lose all those irrational needs and satisfactions which were originated while they were wearing the chains.[22]

Fromm, in fact, holds that the limitations and distortions of consciousness inflicted upon the individual by the society are the primary forms of human alienation. Alienation in awareness is for him more than a reflection of alienation in "real life"; it is the basic form of the problem. Marx is concerned with forced labor; Fromm's central concern is with forced awareness (and forced unawareness). Fromm agrees with Marx that both Hegel and Feuerbach deal with human consciousness only abstractly, not as the product of a particular society; but having learned

21. Cf. Marx and Engels, "The German Ideology," excerpted in *Marx and Engels,* ed. Feuer, pp. 246–260.
22. Fromm, *The Sane Society,* p. 264.

this from Marx, Fromm returns to the non-Marxian view that alienation is primarily a form of awareness or unawareness. The solution to the problem of alienation then will be a state of consciousness as well.

Fromm's position is indicated in his comparison of Freud and Marx on the matter of false consciousness. He holds that both Freud and Marx see man's consciousness as largely "determined by the objective forces which work behind his back." For Freud, these forces are "physiological and biological needs"; for Marx they are "social and economic historical forces."[23] Fromm suggests that for both men freedom from this determination (and the overcoming of alienation) is achieved through increased awareness. "[Man] can attain freedom (and health) only by becoming aware of these motivating forces, that is of reality, and thus he can become the master of his life (within the limitations of reality) rather than the slave of blind forces."[24] Alienation is basically a state of unawareness; productivity and health are achieved through increased awareness of reality within and outside oneself.

In Fromm's view, Freud saw the need for expanding consciousness; but his weakness lay in his failure to perceive that consciousness is shaped by social conditions. Marx saw that the expansion of consciousness can occur only in co-ordination with the achievement of a truly human economic and social order; in Fromm's account there is an interaction between the objectively given conditions of existence in a particular society and the way in which man understands his existence. A significant (or widespread) change in one must be co-ordinated with a change in the other. Fromm considers recognition of the social relativity of human consciousness one of Marx's greatest contributions.

This recognition of relativity did not lead Marx to the position that human nature is itself indeterminate or indefinitely

23. Fromm, *Beyond the Chains of Illusion,* p. 106.
24. *Ibid.,* p. 112.

malleable (nor does it lead Fromm to this position). As the use of such terms as alienation and false consciousness suggest, Marx held that human nature has a certain determinate character which can be realized through the process of social evolution. This theme is prominent in the early writings of Marx; but Fromm maintains that the concept of an essential human nature is assumed throughout the Marxian corpus, although in the later works it is more implicit than explicit. Fromm sees the distinction between man's existence and his essence as a permanent Hegelian element in the viewpoint of Marx.

What Marx does reject is the essence which is a mere "abstraction"—a rootless ideal, a figment of the imagination. He criticized Feuerbach for viewing man's essence in abstraction from the process of history; rather, it is a potentiality in man which can be actualized historically. Fromm paraphrases Marx's *Theses on Feuerbach* in this way:

> The nature (essence) of man can be inferred from its many manifestations (and distortions) in history; it cannot be seen as *such,* as a statistically existing entity "behind" or "above" each separate man, but as that in man which exists as a potentiality and unfolds and changes in the historical process.[25]

This is an adequate expression of Fromm's own view as well. He too holds that man's essence is not identical with his existence but can be inferred from the study of man and his developmental history.

Fromm then is indebted to both Freud and Marx; but in the end the synthesizing process becomes one of incorporating Freudian insights into the general Marxian perspective, rather

25. Fromm, *Marx's Concept of Man,* pp. 78–79. Here is Marx's statement: "Feuerbach resolves the religious essence into the *human* essence. But the human essence is no abstraction inherent in each single individual. In its reality it is the ensemble of the social relations. Feuerbach, who does not enter upon a criticism of this real essence is consequently compelled: (1) To abstract from the historical process and to fix the religious sentiment as something by itself, and to presuppose an abstract-*isolated*-human individual. (2) The human essence, therefore, can with him be comprehended only as 'genus,' as an internal, dumb generality which merely *naturally* unites the many individuals."

than the reverse. Of the two, Fromm considers Marx to be of greater "world historical significance."[26] This is an unfamiliar Marx however: the Marx of the little-known (in America) *Economic and Philosophical Manuscripts* of Marx's Hegelian youth. Fromm holds that this Marx is as misunderstood in the Communist world as he is unknown in the West.

26. Fromm, *Beyond the Chains of Illusion,* p. 12.

fROMM:
scientist or
philosopher?

Fromm's two men-
tors have an ambiguous status in the world of science. Marx and
Freud had utmost confidence in the scientific method, and each
placed his hopes for man's future in the hands of science. But
neither has been accorded undisputed status as a scientist in the
Anglo-American sense. It might be expected, then, that Fromm's
position would be at least equally debatable. In fact, his position
is clear enough, although Fromm makes some claims to the
contrary: Fromm is a philosopher in the final analysis, albeit
a philosopher who makes considerable use of various types of
scientific evidence. This judgment is not an evaluation; it serves
merely to shed some light on the kinds of data with which
Fromm deals and the kind of conclusions which he reaches. Let
us look at the problem more closely.

Fromm and the Science of Man

As we have already suggested, Fromm agrees with Marx that
most of the observable drives and needs of men are socially produced and indefinitely flexible. Most of these psychic needs are
not fixed drives rooted in the biological organism but are relative drives created by the society. Invariant human nature is not
to be found in the "drives which make for the differences in
men's characters, like love and hatred, the lust for power and

the yearning for submission, the enjoyment of sensuous pleasure and the fear of it"; all of these are in fact "products of the social process."[1]

If these empirical data concerning men in particular societies were the only truths about man, no real science of man would, in Fromm's view, be possible. Psychology would be confined to a "radical behaviorism content with describing an infinite number of behavior patterns." And since these patterns would be rooted in the social structure, "there could be but one science of man, comparative sociology."[2]

The ways in which different social structures shape individual character are a concern of Fromm's "psychoanalytic social psychology," as we have seen. This analysis, however, is only one pole in the study of man. It must be co-ordinated with the other pole, namely, research into the essential nature of man. In Fromm's opinion, no true science of man is possible unless man has a nature which can be discovered. "The concept of a science of man rests upon the premise that its object, man, exists and that there is a human nature characteristic of the human species."[3]

This essential nature is not observable as such; it is the task of the science of man to determine the human "core" in all of the various normal and abnormal "manifestations" of human nature. Thus the concept of man becomes a theoretical and ideal construction; but it exists as a real potentiality in man's evolutionary development. Unless this distinction is made, Fromm argues, it becomes impossible to distinguish between real human needs, rooted in the conditions of human existence, and false, artifically produced needs, which feel equally urgent but are in fact unnatural or inhuman.

Is it conceivable that a scientific model of human nature could be constructed on the basis of empirical data? If so, one would expect this construction to be founded upon carefully

1. Fromm, *Escape from Freedom*, p. 12.
2. *Ibid.*, p. 22.
3. Fromm, *Man for Himself*, p. 20.

defined methods of procedure and modes of verification. Fromm, however, has devoted himself primarily to another type of substantiation: he has sought to show that the concept of essential man suggested by certain selected types of psychoanalytic and sociological evidence can be assimilated into the prophetic, Renaissance, and Enlightenment tradition of naturalistic and religious humanism. Indeed, he comes to hold that the vision of the fully "awakened" man is possible only as a philosophical and religious insight.

This radical aim can be envisaged only from the point of view of a certain philosophical position. . . . This aim could not be better described than has been done by Suzuki in terms of the "art of living." One must keep in mind that any such concept as the art of living grows from the soil of a spiritual humanistic orientation, as it underlies the teachings of Buddha, of the prophets, of Jesus, of Meister Eckhart, or of men such as Blake, Walt Whitman, or Bucke.[4]

Is there a reason for Fromm's tendency to gravitate toward philosophical and religious forms of discourse and verification? Fromm has come to feel that the basic method of science as usually understood is inadequate to the task of full awareness, although it is useful in practical pursuits. He views the detachment required by science as a form of alienation which must be overcome (although not eliminated). Man cannot be understood as an object; full knowledge requires participation in the being which is to be known.[5] Science tends to make man into a thing,

4. Fromm, *et al., Zen Buddhism and Psychoanalysis,* p. 136.
5. Cf. *ibid.,* p. 134, and Fromm, *Beyond the Chains of Illusion,* pp. 149–151. Cf. also Fromm, *The Heart of Man,* pp. 116–119: here Fromm makes a distinction which had not been clearly made in his earlier work. He suggests a distinction between the *essence* of human nature and the progressive *goal* of human nature. Here he identifies the essence of man as "life aware of itself," man's self-consciousness and his need for some answer to the problem which this poses. If this distinction were consistently maintained one could say that science can discover the essence of man, but only philosophy and religion can deal adequately with the goals of human existence. In his major works Fromm does not preserve this distinction with any degree of clarity. On the contrary, the term essence connotes a normative concept, and Fromm's usage gravitates in this direction.

and this tendency is one of the great threats to humanism in our time. Thus knowledge of man's nature would be, in contemporary parlance, "existential" knowledge rather than knowledge from detached observation. Fromm has not fully abandoned the claim of being scientific in his methodology, but the contrary tendency is dominant.

Fromm and the Philosophers

Fromm most frequently identifies his position as "humanistic." In *Man for Himself* he associates his viewpoint with humanistic ethics, meaning that in value judgments man must be anthropocentric. He identifies his concept of the "sane society" as normative humanism. In *Zen Buddhism and Psychoanalysis* he seeks to elaborate a "humanistic psychoanalysis."

J. H. Schaar argues, however, that Fromm's humanism "is really naturalism in disguise."[6] Noting that Fromm sees man as discovering the norms for human fulfillment in human nature rather than creating them for himself, Schaar maintains that he can best be described as a naturalist, not a humanist.

According to our analysis, Fromm seeks to overcome the tension between naturalism and humanism in a way fundamentally Hegelian and Marxian. According to Fromm, man is separate from, and opposed to, nature because he is alienated from it. At the same time, however, man represents a further development of nature. In the sane society, when man has become reconciled to nature (and himself), nature itself will have been elevated to a new level. We can look toward a day "when man will have become fully human, and when nature will be humanized as man will be 'naturalized.' "[7] When man's full humanity has been realized, the tension between man and nature will be overcome.

Thus Schaar is correct in affirming that naturalism is Fromm's basic position; but his humanism takes its place within a broader

6. Schaar, *Escape from Authority*, p. 18.
7. Fromm, *et al.*, *Zen Buddhism and Psychoanalysis*, p. 106.

naturalism. Man cannot be truly at home in nature until nature
has been humanized. This development is possible in the
Marxian tradition because of Marx's view that man in creating
himself historically is creating "nature" (in the human sense)
as well. The Hegelian theme of alienation and return ultimately
lies behind Fromm's otherwise unexplained attempt to maintain
both naturalism and humanism.

Fromm appears to stand somewhat apart from the main-
stream of American naturalism. If, as J. H. Randall has suggested, naturalism is characterized essentially by a devotion to
"scientific methods" of interpretation and analysis, it may be
that Fromm's training in the social sciences (as they developed
in Europe under the influence of Marx and Freud) sets him
apart from American naturalism influenced by John Dewey,
whose work was characterized by a "saturation in biological
thought."[8] His attempt to visualize man, a biological and psychic
unity, as the proper object of the science of man leads Fromm
to the quest for a "model of human nature." He criticizes Dewey
for his failure to formulate such a model.

We have noted that this concept of human nature in Fromm's
thought takes on an increasingly religious aspect, though in
naturalistic form. A prominent American naturalist, Sidney
Hook, has distinguished two types of "existential religion": a
theistic existentialism stemming from Soren Kierkegaard, and a
humanistic (or naturalistic) existentialism stemming from Ludwig Feuerbach. According to Hook, Feuerbach, unlike Kierkegaard, preserves Hegel's monism but "naturalizes and demy-
thologizes" the Hegelian system. Hook notes that, although
Kierkegaard's theism has become most influential in the twentieth century, Feuerbach "still awaits his proper recognition."[9]
It would appear that Fromm's work fits Hook's description of
"existentialist religion" in the tradition of Feuerbach.[10]

8. J. H. Randall, Jr., "Epilogue: the Nature of Naturalism," in
Naturalism and the Human Spirit, ed. by Y. H. Krikorian, p. 365.
   9. Sidney Hook, *The Quest for Being*, p. 137.
   10. Tillich, though strongly influenced by Kierkegaard, also preserves
Hegel's monism. One of Tillich's major efforts is to overcome both

Further comments must be made concerning Fromm's relation to existentialism. In *Man for Himself*, Fromm remarks that his terminology is unrelated to the literature of existentialism, with which he professes little acquaintance. In *Marx's Concept of Man,* however, Fromm uses the term "existentialist" to identify the tradition within which Marx stands. "Essentially the whole existentialist philosophy, from Kierkegaard on, is, as Paul Tillich puts it, 'an over one-hundred-years-old movement of rebellion against the dehumanization of man in industrial society.' "[11] Marx's concept of socialism is identified by Fromm as an existentialist protest against alienation. It seems clear that Fromm conceives existentialism along the lines of Tillich's concept, described above; indeed, it is likely that Fromm's view was influenced by that of Tillich. It seems evident that Fromm thinks of himself as belonging to this movement also.

It is no violation of Fromm's position, then, to include him within the existentialist movement, as broadly interpreted by Tillich, and Fromm seems to agree that the concept of alienation is central in the thought of the movement, as Tillich maintains.[12] In this study, we shall, therefore, think of him as an existentialist in Tillich's sense.

One further relationship remains to be mentioned. There are some similarities between Fromm's work and recent elaborations of a "phenomenological" method by various European philosophers. This method consists in a focusing of attention on the structures of the "life-world," of conscious experience. In a recent essay, James Edie explains the main thrust of the movement in this way:

Phenomenology is neither a science of objects nor a science of the subject; it is a science of *experience.* It does not concentrate

---

naturalism and dualistic theism without reproducing Hegel's idealism. We shall seek to determine whether he has succeeded.

11. Fromm, *Marx's Concept of Man,* p. 46. In *The Heart of Man* Fromm disavows any connection with Heidegger and Sartre.

12. Rollo May finds similarities as well as differences in a comparison of Fromm and Kierkegaard: cf. Rollo May, *The Meaning of Anxiety,* pp. 44–45.

exclusively on either the objects of experience or on the subject of experience, but on the point of contact where being and consciousness meet.[13]

Insofar as Fromm concerns himself with the structures of conscious experience, it could be said that he adopts a phenomenological method. This method is implicit, for example, in his critiques of Marxian and Freudian materialism. The life-world, Fromm shows, has its own structures not reducible to physical quantification; but to the extent that Fromm seeks to develop a normative humanism or naturalism, it would appear that he abandons the descriptive and "radically empiricist" method of Husserl and his followers.[14] Fromm, no doubt, could clarify his position further by commenting on his relation to the phenomenologists. We shall have occasion to comment further upon Fromm's approach to consciousness in later sections of our study.

13. James M. Edie, "Introduction," in Pierre Thevenaz, *What is Phenomenology?* ed. by James M. Edie, p. 19.
14. *Ibid.*

V

fROMM's concept of human nature

$F_{ROMM'S}$ thought is given structure by his evolutionary approach to human nature. He sees man as emerging out of a primal unity with nature and moving toward the final goal of productive reunion with nature. Although our central interest is in the intermediate stage—the condition of alienation—this concept can be understood only in the context of Fromm's theories concerning man's origin and his destiny. We must therefore examine Fromm's concepts of the emergence of human nature with its consequent problems and of his solution to these problems.

The Problem of Human Existence: the "Break" with Nature

Fromm begins his analysis of the human situation with the assertion that man, by virtue of his very mode of existence, poses a problem for himself. Human life is not simply a fact to be taken for granted; it is a problem to be solved. The origin of this problem lies in man's original "break" with the unities and harmonies of nature. By beginning the process of becoming human, man has disrupted the harmony of the pre-human state and is now driven to seek new unities and harmonies with nature, his fellow man, and himself.

The problem of man's existence, then, is unique in the whole of nature; he has fallen out of nature, as it were, and is still in it; he is partly divine, partly animal; partly infinite, partly finite. *The necessity to find ever-new solutions for the contradictions in his existence, to find ever-higher forms of unity with nature, his fellow-men and himself, is the source of all psychic forces which motivate man, of all his passions, affects and anxieties.*[1]

Fromm attempts no explanation of this original "break" other than the dynamic of the evolutionary process. He seems to view it as accidental, a product of chance. The break with nature has made man into a strange abnormality, into the "freak of the universe." At the same time, this break can be viewed as the birth of mankind, quite analogous to the birth of an individual man.

From all we know about the evolution of the human race, the birth of man is to be understood in the same sense as the birth of the individual. When man had transcended a certain threshold of minimum instinctive adaptation, he ceased to be an animal; but he was as helpless and unequipped for human existence as the individual infant is at birth. The birth of man began with the first members of the species homo sapiens, and human history is nothing but the process of this birth.[2]

It is apparent that the original break with nature was by no means abrupt. Man in the beginning was still closely bound to "mother nature," and eons had to pass before his distinctive human nature began to emerge. Though the break was not abrupt, it does prevent man from succeeding in any attempt to return to the "womb," to regain the purely animal harmonies.

Man's evolution is based on the fact that he has lost his original home, nature—and that he can never return to it, can never become an animal again.[3]

Fromm begins his anthropology, then, with the premise that man has evolved out of nature, out of an original unity and

1. Fromm, *The Sane Society,* p. 25.
2. *Ibid.,* p. 26.
3. *Ibid.,* p. 25.

harmony that has been irretrievably lost. Once this break has occurred, the dynamic of human development arises out of man's quest for a new unity and harmony. He cannot remain in this state of separation and disequilibrium; he must seek to "find a new relatedness to man and nature after having lost the primary relatedness of the pre-human stage."[4] Human history is a record of this attempt.

Fromm can speak strongly of the negative effects of this original separation.

[Man] is driven to overcome this inner split, tormented by a craving for "absoluteness," for another kind of harmony which can lift the curse by which he was separated from nature, from his fellowmen, and from himself.[5]

He can refer to it in the symbolic terms of "the fall" of man.

Man, who lives in the Garden of Eden, in complete harmony with nature but without awareness of himself, begins his history by the first act of freedom, disobedience to a command. Concomitantly, he becomes aware of himself, of his separateness, of his helplessness; he is expelled from Paradise, and two angels with fiery swords prevent his return.[6]

However, Fromm does not see only negative effects of this "fall," or separation. It is within man's capabilities to move forward toward a higher unity and harmony on a distinctively human level. The only real answer to the human problem is a progressive answer.

There is only one way he can take: to emerge fully from his natural home, to find a new home—one which he creates, by making the world a human one and by becoming truly human himself.[7]

Indeed, it is only by breaking with nature that man can begin to realize his humanity.

We have quoted Fromm as saying that there is only one real

4. *Ibid.*, p. viii.
5. Fromm, *Man for Himself*, p. 41.
6. Fromm, *The Sane Society*, p. 24.
7. *Ibid.*, p. 25.

answer to the human predicament. In fact, however, he sees man torn between two apparent choices: the one, to progress into full humanity, the other, to attempt to regress into the natural harmonies.

We are never free from two conflicting tendencies: one to emerge from the womb, from the animal form of existence into a more human existence, from bondage to freedom; another, to return to the womb, to nature, to certainty and security.[8]

The latter alternative is appealing, but as a solution it necessarily fails. In a broad sense the two alternatives are life and death: to live, in the fullest sense, man must choose the progressive answer.

These alternatives, moreover, are present at every stage in individual or social development, not just in the early stages. A regressive answer is possible at any stage and can take many forms, as we shall see. However, Fromm is confident that, broadly speaking, the progressive tendency has gained the ascendancy in the history of the race.

Fromm makes a distinction between the regressive answer to life (which is his reinterpretation of Freud's "death-wish") and the *acceptance* of the fact of physical death. He holds that denial of the "tragic fact that man's life ends in death" is only self-deception or a false ideology. In fact, the refusal to accept the reality of death would have to be termed a regressive attitude, since it denies the truth about existence. Fromm seems to be saying that death is basically antithetical to life, and cannot be incorporated into a philosophy of life. Yet one who denies death does not really accept life. Though man must recognize the limits of finite existence, it is still possible to move forward toward the full realization of the "specifically human potentiality of reason and love."[9] Fromm's interest centers on the removal of pathological blocks to this mature fulfillment. These, and not physical death, are man's "problem." These blocks can be re-

8. *Ibid.*, p. 27.
9. Fromm, *et al.*, *Zen Buddhism and Psychoanalysis*, p. 94.

moved; the problem of physical death cannot be solved and thus is not a genuine problem. The problems connected with man's separation from nature are apparently not, in his view, essentially related to the fact of physical death.

Some clarification of the concept of the "break" with nature is now necessary. Fromm holds that the break coincides with the advent of self-consciousness.

I have said that man is asked a question by the very fact of his existence, and that this is a question raised by the contradiction within himself—that of being in nature and at the same time of transcending nature by the fact that he is life aware of itself.[10]

Fromm makes a distinction, for which he gives credit to R. M. Bucke, between "simple," or animal, consciousness, and human consciousness, which contains self-consciousness, man's "awareness of himself as the subject of his experience."[11] Fromm seems elsewhere to use consciousness and self-consciousness interchangeably, apparently implying that self-consciousness is present as a component in all human awareness once it is achieved by the individual child. It is awareness of himself as a separate entity that lifts man out of nature into a new level of existence.

This kind of consciousness is a complex phenomenon. Its achievement is contingent upon a social development, namely the development of a "conceptual system," a set of "categories." Though Fromm concedes that some of these categories may be universal and common to all men, his emphasis is placed on the fact that in large measure the conceptual system is the product of a social evolution.

This [conceptual] system is in itself a result of social evolution. Every society, by its own practice of living and by the mode of relatedness, of feeling, of perceiving, develops a system of categories which determines the forms of awareness.[12]

The development of human consciousness and the role of society

10. *Ibid.*, p. 92.
11. *Ibid.*, p. 98.
12. *Ibid.*, p. 99.

in fostering the development and limiting the content of consciousness will be examined more closely in our analysis of alienation. Suffice it to say here that for Fromm the "birth" of man and self-consciousness cannot be separated from the "birth" of society, and that both of these births are gradual evolutionary processes.

Making the Unconscious Conscious

We have spoken of the break with nature and have identified it with the advent of self-consciousness. We turn now to a consideration of Fromm's view of the "goal" of human nature. Though Fromm does speak of man as the "freak of the universe," he takes the view that man has a potential human nature which can be realized, a realization toward which the break with nature is a positive step. We have seen that man's birth prevents his returning to the pre-human unity with nature, except in insanity or death. This separation, however, is only in consciousness; by becoming conscious man has not lost the possibility of a new unity with nature. All levels of nature are still present in him, but they are simply below the level of conscious awareness.

But man, in any culture, has all the potentialities: he is the archaic man, the beast of prey, the cannibal, the idolater, and he is the being with the capacity for reason, for love, for justice. The content of the unconscious, then, is neither the good nor the evil, the rational nor the irrational; it is both; it is all that is human. The unconscious is the whole man—minus that part of man which corresponds to his society. Consciousness represents social man, the accidental limitations set by the historical situation into which an individual is thrown. Unconsciousness represents universal man, the whole man, rooted in the Cosmos; it represents the plant in him, the animal in him, the spirit in him; it represents his past down to the dawn of human existence, and it represents his future to the day when man will have become fully human, and when nature will be humanized as man will be "naturalized." [13]

13. *Ibid.*, p. 106.

Thus the whole man is a microcosm containing all nature within himself.

But conscious man has become separated from these roots in the Cosmos. This separation results from the failure of certain feelings and experiences to emerge into consciousness (for various reasons, as we shall see). In Fromm's view, one way of expressing the goal of human nature, then, is the goal of making the unconscious conscious. Since this achievement is the goal of human existence, it is also the goal of Fromm's "humanistic psychoanalysis."

> The most characteristic element in the psychoanalytic approach is, without any doubt, its attempt *to make the unconscious conscious* —or, to put it in Freud's words, to transform Id into Ego.[14]

According to Fromm, this goal had a limited function for Freud: the control of the repressed impulses of the unconscious by the ego. Fromm visualizes a broader application of the idea.

> When we free ourselves from the limited concept of Freud's unconscious . . . then Freud's aim, the transformation of unconsciousness into consciousness ("Id into Ego") gains a wider and more profound meaning. *Making the unconscious conscious transforms the mere idea of the universality of man into a living experience of this universality; it is the experiential realization of humanism.*[15]

When full consciousness is achieved man experiences himself once again as in unity with nature; the "break" is overcome.

The Productive Orientation

Fromm describes the goal of human nature in other terms. His concept of the distinctive potentialities of human nature can best be summarized in his concept of the "productive orientation."

In discussing the productive character I venture beyond critical analysis and inquire into the nature of fully developed character

14. *Ibid.,* p. 95.
15. *Ibid.,* p. 107.

that is the aim of human development and simultaneously the ideal of humanistic ethics.[16]

The "productive orientation" is a total configuration of character, a mode of relating to the world and to oneself which employs one's inherent powers.

The productive orientation of personality refers to a fundamental attitude, a mode of relatedness in all realms of human experience. It covers mental, emotional and sensory responses to others, to oneself, and to things. Productiveness is man's ability to use his powers and to realize the potentialities inherent in him.[17]

Fromm speaks of three "powers" or "modes of relatedness" which represent the realization of that which is distinctively human: reason, love, and creativity.

With his power of reason [man] can penetrate the surface of phenomena and understand their essence. With his power of love he can break through the wall which separates one person from another. With his power of imagination he can visualize things not yet existing; he can plan and thus begin to create.[18]

Thus the productive orientation in these three ways overcomes man's separation from nature, his fellow men, and himself, and it is, at the same time, a realization of his inherent potentialities.

Since Fromm's understanding of the power of reason will be discussed below, and since his concept of creativity is not well developed and is largely implicit in the broader concept of productivity, some comments might be made here concerning Fromm's treatment of love.

Fundamentally, love is for Fromm the reunion of the separated, the overcoming of alienation.

The necessity to unite with other living beings, to be related to them, is an imperative need on the fulfillment of which man's sanity depends. This need is behind all phenomena which constitute the whole gamut of intimate human relations, of all passions which are called love in the broadest sense of the word.[19]

16. Fromm, *Man for Himself*, p. 83.
17. *Ibid.*, p. 84.
18. *Ibid.*, p. 88.
19. Fromm, *The Sane Society*, p. 30.

Immediately, however, it is necessary to distinguish two basic types of reunion and, correspondingly, two types of love. There are first the regressive forms of reunion. Many of these forms appear to be relationships of love, but in reality they are types of dominance or submission, "symbiotic" relationships which do not satisfy man's real need. Genuine love is a form of union which preserves the integrity of the lovers. "Love is *union* with somebody, or something, outside oneself, under the condition of retaining the separateness and integrity of one's own self." [20] Genuine love, then, within the framework of our analysis, is progressive, rather than regressive, union. Fromm criticizes Freud for viewing all forms of union as regressive narcissism; he holds that union is possible on a mature level.

Our main interest here is in Fromm's concept of mature love. It would seem that in discussing "progressive" love Fromm alternates between two partially contradictory conceptions. On the one hand, as we have seen, progressive (as well as regressive) love springs from man's deep need to be reunited with the world and his fellow man. This understanding suggests that love presupposes alienation, that union presupposes separation.

On the other hand, Fromm describes love as a form of productivity. Love is self-giving, the highest expression of human potency.

In the very act of giving, I experience my strength, my wealth, my power. This experience of heightened vitality and potency fills me with joy. I experience myself as overflowing, spending, alive, hence as joyous. Giving is more joyous than receiving, not because it is a deprivation, but because in the act of giving lies the expression of my aliveness.[21]

Fromm understands the traditional concept of God's generous and overflowing love for man as a symbol for man's productive love.

The human reality behind the concept of man's love for God in humanistic religion is man's ability to love productively, to love

20. *Ibid.*, p. 31.
21. Fromm, *The Art of Loving*, p. 23.

without greed, without submission and domination, to love from the fullness of his personality, just as God's love is a symbol for love out of strength and not out of weakness.[22]

In these descriptions Fromm seems to view love as arising, not from need, but from a spontaneous overflow of vitality or activity.

If our analysis of Fromm is correct, productive love in the sense just described must be the fruit of reunion, not its source. If love is a form of productivity, it is exactly the separated or alienated man who cannot love in the mature sense. He is severed from the source of such potency. On the other hand, the productive individual has no need for reunion; he has already achieved "a new relatedness to man and nature." He loves as an expression of his own aliveness, not out of any kind of drivenness or passion. It would appear that Fromm must choose between two concepts: love as need, and love as overflowing vitality. He cannot maintain both that the act of reunion is a productive act, and that productivity stems from a person who has achieved reunion.[23]

In fact, it is doubtful that love is the primary path to reunion for Fromm, especially in his later work. In his developing perspective, as we shall see in more detail, the alienated man has lost touch with his own nature; the man who rediscovers humanity and nature within himself can then love humanity and life in others. This comes, not through love, but through "de-repression." The man who has overcome repressedness can say: "I am in touch with the deepest sources within myself, and that means with all of humanity. . . . inasmuch as I am not a stranger to myself, no one and nothing is a stranger to me."[24] Reunion for Fromm occurs first of all within oneself, and then with the neighbor. It is true that the rediscovery of self may be a form of self-

22. Fromm, *Psychoanalysis and Religion*, p. 87.
23. We might say that Fromm has sought to combine two different motifs: the *erōs* motif and the *agapé* motif. It is doubtful that they can be combined in this way.
24. Fromm, *et al.*, *Zen Buddhism and Psychoanalysis*, p. 127.

love; and this Fromm approves, so long as it is in correlation with one's love of his neighbor. However, this love must also be productive—and not narcissistic. The original motive to be reunited with the fullness of one's own nature must be for Fromm the inexplicable progressive impulse of nature to which we have referred, rather than love.

One other important characteristic of productivity in Fromm's account is freedom. Fromm distinguishes two ways of understanding human freedom: a negative understanding and a positive understanding, "freedom from" and "freedom to." [25] Fromm views the former as the release from natural and traditional bondages. Though he does not mention it here, the original break with nature, it would seem, could be considered the beginning of "freedom from." Fromm refers to being "freed from traditional authorities," apparently a reference to the authority of mother, father, clan, etc., over the not-yet-matured individual. History records the gradual emergence of individuality, as man frees himself from these traditional bonds (here again by analogy with individual growth and development).

But this state of negative freedom is an insecure and frightening condition which cannot long be endured.

At the same time [man] has become isolated, powerless, and an instrument of purposes outside of himself, alienated from himself and others; furthermore—this state undermines his self, weakens and frightens him and makes him ready for submission to new kinds of bondage.[26]

This state is untenable, that is, unless it is accompanied by positive freedom, "freedom to." And this is none other than the power to express one's own nature, to realize one's inherent potentialities. "Positive freedom on the other hand is identical with the full realization of the individual's potentialities, together with his ability to live actively and spontaneously." [27]

25. Fromm, *Escape from Freedom,* p. 32.
26. *Ibid.,* p. 270.
27. *Ibid.*

Thus freedom in the positive sense is equivalent to "productivity."

We must now seek to show the relationship between the goal of "making the unconscious conscious" and that of the "productive orientation." Fromm assures us that they are closely related.

The full awakening to reality means, again speaking in psychological terms, to have attained a fully "productive orientation." That means not to relate oneself to the world receptively, exploitatively, hoardingly, or in the marketing fashion, but creatively, actively (in Spinoza's sense). In the state of full productiveness there are no veils which separate me from the "not me." [28]

It must be admitted that although Fromm affirms the essential identity of these two concepts he nowhere establishes this identity through detailed analysis. It is, however, partly implicit in the concept of consciousness which he has elaborated in several works.

For Fromm, consciousness is a mode of relatedness, and hence a mode of activity (not simply receptivity). This active view of consciousness Fromm finds in the early Marx. "Consciousness," said Marx, "can never be anything else than conscious existence, and the existence of men is their actual life process." [29] Both Marx and Fromm however must distinguish between true consciousness and false consciousness; Marx is willing to say in this same passage that man's consciousness is determined by the modes of material production and exchange. When there is no forced labor, one might say, there will be no false consciousness. By the same token, for Fromm, when there is no forced awareness there will be no false awareness. Thus when consciousness is a self-activity, not a form of passivity, it will be both true and productive.

We have noted a certain similarity between Fromm's thought and recent phenomenological research. This similarity is notable

28. Fromm, *et al.*, *Zen Buddhism and Psychoanalysis*, p. 116.
29. Marx and Engels, "The German Ideology," excerpted in *Marx and Engels*, ed. by Feuer, p. 247.

in Fromm's approach to consciousness. In comparing the pragmatism of William James with contemporary phenomenology James Edie writes:

The primacy of *action* as the fundamental category of early pragmatism gives us a notion of man-in-the-world, of an incarnate, unitary intentional consciousness continuous with the notion of an intentionality of consciousness which is the basic discovery of phenomenology. Consciousness is less a type of "seeing" than of "acting." It is *praxis* before it can become *theoria*.[30]

It is clear that Fromm shares this general viewpoint.[31] Thus the disparity between the concepts of full consciousness and productivity is reduced, if not entirely eliminated.

The goal of human nature, then, as we have seen, can be variously described as productiveness, full awareness, freedom, a new relatedness based on love, reason, and creativity. All of these qualities are simply aspects of the actualization of human potentiality. In fact, in Fromm's view, all genuine human "activity," stemming from the individual as "actor," leads toward this actualization. Fromm identifies his concept of activity with that of Spinoza.

One concept of activity, the modern one, refers to the use of energy for the achievement of external aims; the other concept of activity refers to the use of man's inherent powers, regardless of whether any external change is brought about. The latter concept of activity has been formulated most clearly by Spinoza. He differentiates among the affects between active and passive affects, "actions" and "passions." In the exercise of an active affect, man is free, he is the master of his affect; in the exercise of a passive affect, man is driven, the object of motivations of which he is not aware.[32]

For Fromm all genuine "activity" is thus virtuous (produc-

30. Pierre Thevanaz, *What is Phenomenology?* ed. with introduction by James M. Edie, p. 35.
31. One important difference would appear to be that phenomenology is a "radical empiricism" and detects many different kinds of "life-worlds." Fromm holds that full consciousness discovers the one real world as it truly is. Perhaps at this point he is more Hegelian than Kantian.
32. Fromm, *The Art of Loving*, pp. 21–22.

tive). Evil is passivity, submission, "escape from freedom"; it is merely the absence of good, productivity.

We have shown that man is not necessarily evil but becomes evil only if the proper conditions for his growth and development are lacking. The evil has no independent existence of its own, it is the absence of good. It is the result of the failure to realize life.[33]

Fromm suggests that in the humanistic religions God is a symbol for the full realization of human powers. Of humanistic religion, he writes:

God is not a symbol of power over man but of man's own powers.

.   .   .   .

in humanistic religion God is the image of man's higher self, a symbol of what man potentially is or ought to become.[34]

Thus the goal of human nature is not an externally imposed standard but the fulfillment of the potentialities of man's own nature.

The Problem of Regression

One important question remains unanswered in this account of Fromm's concept of "productivity" or "activity." In what sense are regressive impulses an original and permanent part of human nature? Would it be possible to speak of regressive "activity," or can regression in fact always be understood as "passivity"? This question takes on some importance in Fromm's work, for if certain natural human impulses are incurably self-destructive, then they ought to be repressed and excluded from the conscious self, thus defeating the purpose of "making the unconscious conscious." Fromm has apparently had some difficulty with this question, for different answers to it can be discerned in his work.

At times Fromm seems to hold that progressive and regressive impulses exist simultaneously in the individual. After stat-

33. Fromm, *Man for Himself,* p. 218.
34. Fromm, *Psychoanalysis and Religion,* p. 49.

ing that "we are never free from two conflicting tendencies,"
Fromm in a footnote adds this comment:

> It is in this polarity that I see the true kernel in Freud's hy-
> pothesis of the existence of a life and death instinct; the difference
> to Freud's theory is, that the forward-going and the retrogressive
> impulse have not the same biologically determined strength, but that
> normally, the forward-going life instinct is stronger and increases
> in relative strength the more it grows.[35]

This same view, that man possesses two opposing "instincts,"
seems to be supported in a later passage. After speaking of the
role of society in encouraging repression (an idea which we shall
examine later), Fromm writes of a different kind of repression:

> We tend also to repress those strivings which are incompatible
> with the principle of structure and growth of the whole human
> being, incompatible with the "humanistic conscience," that voice
> which speaks in the name of the full development of our person.[36]

Regressive impulses, he writes, "are under no circumstances
compatible with the inherent goals of the evolution of man's
nature."[37]

If these statements represent Fromm's final position on this
subject, it would seem that his view of productivity outlined
above would have to be somewhat modified. Only the productive impulses can be permitted; others must be repressed. Repression is a necessary evil; and man remains a divided being,
indeed, an alienated being, in Fromm's sense of the word.
Nature itself (in man) is divided against itself. This view is more
in keeping with that of Freud.

But Fromm seemingly does not consistently maintain this
position. A major theme of his later work is the importance of
complete "de-repression."

> To the degree to which repressedness diminishes, I am in touch
> with the deepest sources within myself, and that means with all of

35. Fromm, *The Sane Society*, p. 27n.
36. Fromm, *et al.*, *Zen Buddhism and Psychoanalysis*, pp. 104–105.
37. *Ibid.*, p. 105.

humanity. If all repressedness has been lifted, there is no more unconscious as against conscious; there is direct, immediate experience.[38]

In an earlier work, Fromm states his opposition to the split
between reason and nature, a split which would seem in this
passage to correspond to the later distinction between the conscious and the unconscious:

One premise for this spontaneity [i.e., productivity] is the acceptance of the total personality and the elimination of the split between
"reason" and "nature"; for only if man does not repress essential
parts of his self, only if he has become transparent to himself, and
only if the different spheres of life have reached a fundamental inte-
gration, is spontaneous activity possible.[39]

Also, Fromm explicitly rejects Freud's view that civilization is
necessarily built upon repression.

In his discussion of destructiveness, which he understands as
a form of regression, Fromm seems to suggest an alternative
approach to the question. He here asserts that destructiveness
(and hence, by implication, other regressive impulses) is a kind
of secondary potentiality, which emerges only if the primary
potentiality is thwarted. Man becomes destructive only if he
cannot be productive; the two modes of life are mutually exclu-
sive. "[Destructiveness] is only the *alternative* to creativeness.
Creation and destruction, love and hate, are not two instincts
which exist independently."[40]

If we follow this approach, however, another question arises:
whence comes the blockage which transmutes creativeness into
destructiveness? The obvious answer is society, and there is
some indication in Fromm's work that this is indeed his answer.
Undoubtedly society for Fromm can, and frequently does,
function in a repressive manner, causing such a blockage. We
will want to examine this role of society in some detail later on.
The question here is whether, in Fromm's view, regressive

38. *Ibid.,* p. 127.
39. Fromm, *Escape from Freedom,* pp. 258–259.
40. Fromm, *The Sane Society,* p. 38.

society can be set over against progressive man in an unambiguous manner. Does Fromm hold that regressive impulses, which have no "primary" roots in human nature, can come to dominate a society?

It is true that Fromm's emphasis is upon the negative effect of society on the fulfillment of individuals. Will Herberg, in an analysis of Fromm, concludes on the basis of this emphasis that Fromm locates the source of evil (or regression) solely in society as an entity which stands over against man's true interests. Herberg writes:

Fromm's interest in history, like Rousseau's, is to lay bare the many ways in which evil institutions have corrupted man in the past, and to draw appropriate lessons from the story. . . . For him, "sin" is socially derived, and history is redeemable through human effort.[41]

It might be argued, however, that this is a one-sided interpretation of Fromm's work. We have noted (and will examine in more detail) Fromm's view that society goes through a course of development analogous to the growth of individuals. Societies can, like individuals, be infantile and regressive; indeed the development of sane and mature individuals partly awaits the achievement of the sane society. The achievement of the sane society, however, awaits the leadership of mature individuals. Fromm thinks of the founders of the great religions as the pathfinders for humanity. Men of vision can lead a society to break new ground in the direction of human fulfillment. On the other hand, individuals can become regressive against the dominant tone of the culture. After pointing out that a regressive religion may seem reasonable by being shared, he writes: "When it is not shared, when the regressive wishes are in contrast to consciousness and the claims of the existing culture, then the secret, individual 'religion' is a neurosis."[42] It is fair to say that Fromm's

41. Will Herberg, "Freud and the Revisionists," in *Freud and the Twentieth Century,* ed. by Benjamin Nelson, pp. 156–157.
42. Fromm, *et al., Zen Buddhism and Psychoanalysis,* p. 91.

interest lies more in the analysis of the "socially patterned defects" than of the neurosis, but both are regressive. Fromm tends to think of humanity (or cultural segments thereof) as a growing organism; finally, the individual and the society cannot be separated. We must locate the source of regression in man, in human impulses, not in something which stands over against man. The blockage referred to earlier may be directly due to the influence of society on the individual; but society becomes regressive because this impulse is somehow rooted in human nature.

If we concede the original existence of regressive impulses, other alternatives for dealing with them appear in Fromm's work. At some points Fromm seems to suggest that instead of repressing the regressive impulses they may properly be redirected toward oneself. For example, concerning impulses to remain dependent upon father or mother, Fromm writes:

In the process of maturing, the conscience becomes more and more independent from these original father and mother figures; *we become,* as it were, *our own father and . . . mother,* and . . . *child.*[43]

With regard to religion, Fromm suggests that one might experience "being God."[44] Fromm seems to be alluding here to his view of man as a being who contains all aspects of nature within himself. However, the discovery of the fact of his "universality" occurs *after* the overcoming of narcissism, not before. A narcissistic or regressive return to the self would be destructive. This redirection of regressive impulses toward the self assumes that regression has, in fact, already been overcome.

Still another attitude toward regressive impulses can be discovered in Fromm's work. At times he suggests the view that regressive impulses will wither away and die out as the progressive impulses are encouraged. In comparing the ethical attitudes of Zen Buddhism and humanistic psychoanalysis, Fromm writes:

43. Fromm, *The Sane Society,* p. 47.
44. Fromm, *et al., Zen Buddhism and Psychoanalysis,* p. 92.

They do not tend to make a man lead a virtuous life by the suppression of the "evil" desire, but they expect that the evil desire will melt away and disappear under the light and warmth of enlarged consciousness.[45]

It would seem legitimate here to identify "evil desire" with regressive desire. In speaking of the function of humanistic conscience (which Fromm interprets as knowledge of the goal of human nature), he writes: "His conscience ought to tell him which needs to cultivate and satisfy and which needs to let wither and starve out."[46] We might refer also to the passage which indicates Fromm's view that the progressive impulse is the stronger.

It would appear that Fromm as yet has no final answer to the question of the relation between regressive impulses and man's basic nature, although the one cited in the last paragraph is perhaps most in keeping with the basic structure of his work.[47] He is impressed with the recurrent strength of regressive impulses in human history at a stage when, according to his theory of historical development, they should have been overcome.[48] At the same time, he is confident that life actively lived is inherently progressive. The main tenor of his work seems to imply that the regressive impulse (or the "death-wish") is not an ineradicable instinct in human nature. It can be overcome, and perhaps eliminated, through the power of consciousness, through a social and historical process. Man becomes alienated, as we shall see, as a necessary consequence of the development of consciousness, through the instrumentality of society. Alienation can finally be viewed in Fromm's thought as a progressive, though frightening, step. It is a dangerous stage in human development, however, because it can lead to the regressive reaction which we have described. Since Fromm has not been com-

45. *Ibid.*, p. 123.
46. Fromm, *The Sane Society*, p. 28.
47. This general view is restated in Fromm's *The Heart of Man*, pp. 121–123.
48. Cf., for example, his study of Nazism in *Escape from Freedom*.

pletely successful in explaining the power of the regressive impulse, he has not given a clear explanation of the circumstance under which alienation leads to regression; but it is clear that regression is a *reaction* to potential or actual alienation. To an examination of this concept we now turn.

alienation

$\mathbf{W}$E HAVE discussed Fromm's view of man's original "break" with nature, and his understanding of human history as the process of "birth" of the human race, quite analogous to the birth of an individual man. History is seen as an extension of nature, moving through stages of growth toward the full realization of human potentialities. To achieve this realization, a negative possibility must be overcome: the possibility of regression toward the original state of unity with nature, a possibility which leads to "death" rather than "life."

In Fromm's analysis, however, the growth of man toward the positive "goal" of human nature, either in an individual or in the race, is not a unilinear evolutionary ascent from a lower form of life. Man's unique nature is such that in order to realize himself fully as an individual he must first separate himself from nature and his fellow man, and in a real sense from himself. He must go out from his "home" in nature and see himself as a distinct and separate entity before he can be reunited with nature, his fellow man, and himself, on a higher, conscious level. He must, in a word, become alienated; full realization lies on the other side of alienation. Fromm states this most clearly in connection with his interpretation of progressive religions:

Unity is sought in all these religions—not the regressive unity found by going back to the pre-individual, preconscious harmony of paradise, but unity on a new level: that unity which can be arrived at only after man has experienced his separateness, after he has gone through the stage of alienation from himself and from the world, and has been fully born.[1]

Or again, in describing the view of Hegel and Marx, Fromm states: "Man has to become alienated in order to overcome this split in the activity of his reason. The same holds true for love."[2]

In these passages, Fromm uses the term alienation to apply to a necessary stage in the movement toward maturity, involving one's awareness of oneself as a separate individual. He emphasizes that this awareness, achieved through alienation, is not lost in full maturity and reconciliation.

Well-being means to be fully related to man and nature affectively, to overcome separateness and alienation, to arrive at the experience of oneness with all that exists, and yet to experience *myself* at the same time as the separate entity *I* am, as the individual.[3]

Alienation and Regression

We will want to examine this progressive view of alienation in more detail. It must first be noted, however, that Fromm does not always use the term "alienation" in this sense. In fact, the view described here seems to have clearly emerged only in his later work. In more recent writing he clarifies a distinction which he had not made clear earlier: the distinction between alienation as such and the regressive answer to the problem posed by the fact of alienation. At times Fromm seems to identify alienation with the regressive answer to alienation, though the latter is really a form of reunion. This inconsistency can best be illustrated in Fromm's treatment of religion. He understands religions as attempts to answer the problem of human existence. "Religion is the formalized and elaborate answer to man's existence."[4] However, religions may give two fundamentally

1. Fromm, *et al., Zen Buddhism and Psychoanalysis*, p. 94.
2. Fromm, *Beyond the Chains of Illusion*, p. 57.
3. Fromm, *et al., Zen Buddhism and Psychoanalysis*, p. 91.
4. *Ibid.*, p. 91.

different answers to man's problem: the progressive and the regressive answers.

But it is deceptive to think of religions as if they had, necessarily, something in common beyond the concern with giving *an* answer to the question of existence. As far as the *content* of religion is concerned, there is no unity whatsoever; on the contrary there are two fundamentally opposite answers.

. . . .

One answer is to go back to prehuman, preconscious existence, to do away with reason, to become an animal and thus to become one with nature again.

. . . .

The other pole of religion is represented by all those religions which seek the answer to the question of human existence by emerging fully from prehuman existence, by developing the specifically human potentiality of reason and love and thus by finding a new harmony between man and nature—and between man and man.[5]

Now it is clear in Fromm's account that idolatrous religion is one form of the regressive answer to the problem of human existence. Yet Fromm clearly identifies alienation and idolatry. In his fullest treatment of the idea of alienation he states:

The concept [alienation] is a much older one; it is the same to which the prophets of the Old Testament referred as *idolatry*.

. . . .

Every act of submissive worship is an act of alienation and idolatry in this sense.[6]

Elsewhere, Fromm identifies alienation with authoritarian religion (as contrasted with humanistic, progressive religion). "The real fall of man is his alienation from himself, his submission to power, his turning against himself even though under the guise of his worship of God."[7]

It would appear that in Fromm's later work, alienation is

5. *Ibid.*, pp. 92–94.
6. Fromm, *The Same Society*, pp. 121–123.
7. Fromm, *Psychoanalysis and Religion*, p. 53.

mainly identified with what Fromm earlier called "the problem of human existence." In *The Sane Society* Fromm describes the human predicament in this fashion:

Man is torn away from the primary union with nature, which characterizes animal existence. Having at the same time reason and imagination, he is aware of his aloneness and separateness; of his powerlessness and ignorance; of the accidentalness of his birth and of his death. He could not face this state of being for a second if he could not find new ties with his fellow man which replace the old ones, regulated by instincts. Even if all his physiological needs were satisfied, he would experience his state of aloneness and individuation as a prison from which he had to break out in order to retain his sanity.[8]

This would appear to be an accurate description of what he later calls alienation. On the other hand, as we have seen, phenomena which are earlier termed alienation he now describes as regressive answers to the problem of human existence.

The relation between alienation and regression, however, is more complex than is immediately apparent. We have been speaking of alienation as equivalent to awareness of oneself as an individual, but self-awareness is itself a complex phenomenon. In order to clarify Fromm's analysis, we might suggest a distinction between the form of consciousness (or abstract consciousness) and the content of consciousness. Man, because of the unique characteristics of his brain, has the formal or abstract capacity for consciousness. However, the actual content of consciousness (that is, how self and world are understood) is deeply affected by the type of society into which the individual is born. A regressive society, as we shall see, may force the individual to repress some aspects of his own self-awareness. As we have seen, it is the limitation of the content of consciousness that must be eliminated in full maturity. Since this limitation is due in large measure to the *repressive* effect of society on the individual, and since this in turn stems from *regression* in society,

8. Fromm, *The Sane Society,* p. 30.

we can see that alienation and regression cannot be completely separated, though they must be distinguished.

It would seem fair to say that the term *alienation* is not best applied to the regressive answers, for these answers presuppose alienation as the human problem. We conclude that Fromm's later use of the term is more appropriate: the description of man's separateness and aloneness because of self-awareness. However, it is not self-awareness as such which represents alienation, but only a limited self-awareness. We must at this point describe in more detail the development of self-consciousness, as presented in Fromm's account.

Alienation and Self-awareness

We have spoken of man's "break" with nature and have identified it with the "birth" of the individual and the race. Fromm uses birth in a broader sense, however, than merely physical birth. The latter is only the beginning of human birth. The physical birth of an infant is not a radical break with the "pre-human harmonies." The newborn infant has no awareness of himself as separate and distinct from his environment.

For the infant shortly after birth, there is not even awareness of reality existing outside of himself in the sense of sense-perception. He and mother's nipple and mother's breasts are still one; he finds himself in a state *before* any subject-object differentiation takes place.[9]

To describe the process of achieving self-awareness we must distinguish three of its aspects. First we must trace two parallel but partially independent developments within the individual: the development of objectivity, or what Fromm sometimes calls "intellection," and the development of "overcoming narcissism." Then we must show the effect of society in limiting and/or distorting the consciousness of individuals.

We have already referred to the necessity of a "conceptual system," without which no experience can enter conscious

9. Fromm, *et al., Zen Buddhism and Psychoanalysis,* p. 89.

awareness. Even after the child has learned to make a minimal use of this system, he does not think of himself as separate from his experience.

For the new-born infant there is as yet no separation between the me and the not-me. This separation takes place, and the final achievement is expressed by the fact that the child can say "I." But still the child's grasp of the world remains relatively immediate and direct. When the child plays with a ball it really sees a ball moving, it is fully *in* this experience, and that is why it is an experience which can be repeated without end, and with a never ceasing joy.[10]

As the person matures and his intellect develops, he begins to see himself as separate from the world which he experiences. Fromm refers to this development as the "split between subject and object." He raises the question whether this achievement is the same as consciousness. He concludes that a kind of consciousness is possible which overcomes the subject-object split. Therefore, a distinction must be made between consciousness as such and "intellectual reflection."

Intellectual reflection is, of course, always conscious, but not all that is conscious is intellectual reflection. If I look at a person, I am *aware* of the person, I am aware of whatever happens to me in relation to the person, but only if I have separated myself from him in a subject-object distance is this consciousness identical with intellectual reflection.[11]

Nonreflective consciousness appears on the far side of alienation and represents man's reunion with the world.

The development of intellectual reflection or the subject-object split is a necessary part of the achievement of rationality and, of course, is especially useful in scientific and practical pursuits. At the same time, however, it leads to alienation. Fromm states:

10. *Ibid.,* p. 128; as we shall see, Fromm takes this "pre-intellectual, immediate grasp of the child" as a model for the "enlightenment" experience which lies on the other side of "the full development of man's reason, objectivity, individuality."
11. *Ibid.,* p. 97.

To be aware of my breathing does not mean *to think about* my breathing. To be aware of the movement of my hand does not mean to think about it. On the contrary, once I *think about* my breathing or the movement of my hand, I am not any more aware of my breathing or of the movement of my hand. The same holds true of my awareness of a flower or a person, of my experience of joy, love, or peace.[12]

In intellection, experience has lost its immediacy.

Closely related to the development of intellection is the use of language. Experiences cannot usually emerge into consciousness unless a word is available to describe them. But as soon as an experience is reduced to words a separation occurs. Certain language styles may produce this type of alienated experience more than others.

This general process of cerebration is more widespread and intense in modern culture than it probably was at any time before in history. Just because of the increasing emphasis on intellectual knowledge which is a condition for scientific and technical achievements, and in connection with it on literacy and education, words more and more take the place of experience.[13]

What Fromm says here about language is apparently related to his view of the "conceptual system," mentioned earlier. Experience can be organized and categorized in various ways, according to the culture. Some cultures emphasize "the purely intellectual side of knowledge" to the exclusion of the "affective" side. (This function of culture is related to but should be distinguished from the repressive function to be discussed.)

We might refer again to the distinction between the form of consciousness and the content of consciousness. Self-world awareness as such is not alienation; consciousness is not necessarily separation; but formal consciousness is not possible without specific content, and this content is organized by the "conceptual system" and by language. These two phenomena are cultural products. As such they may, while enabling men to be

12. *Ibid.*, p. 132.
13. *Ibid.*, p. 109.

conscious at all, fail at the same time to bring certain aspects of experience into awareness, thus alienating men from the fullness of their natures and potential experiences. An intellectualizing culture, for example, may fail to develop ways for expressing affective experiences.

The second major aspect of the process of achieving self-awareness is the overcoming of narcissism. We have noted that the ability to view the world as separate from oneself develops only gradually. In the normally maturing individual this development is accompanied by the growing ability to accept reality as such, and not as one would wish it to be. This is primarily an emotional, or affective development, rather than an intellectual one.

In an *affective* sense, it takes the development of full maturity to overcome the narcissistic attitude of omniscience and omnipotence, provided this stage is ever reached. . . . In the normal development of the child this [narcissistic] attitude slowly changes to the mature one of being aware of reality and accepting it, its laws, hence necessity. In the neurotic person we find invariably that he has not arrived at this point. . . . He insists that reality must conform to his ideas.[14]

Fromm implies that one might have the ability of intellectual reflection fully developed, and yet remain emotionally dependent and infantile. Narcissism is closely related to regression, which we have already discussed. Perhaps a distinction could be made by referring to narcissism as pre-alienation, and regression as post-alienation in sequence. Narcissism is natural at an infant's stage of development but not for an adult. It might be noted that Fromm uses the term "maturity" in the above passage in reference to an alienated condition. The overcoming of narcissism leaves man mature in one sense, but separate and isolated unless he can move forward to a new unity on the other side of alienation.

The third aspect to be discussed in the process of achieving self-awareness is the role of society in determining the content

14. *Ibid.,* p. 90.

of consciousness. We have seen how the use of any language, while necessary for awareness of experiences, leads to an alienation from the immediacy of experience. Furthermore, the language of a particular society may lead to a greater or lesser degree of alienation, depending upon its emphasis on intellection. Beyond this, however, the whole mode of life and attitude toward life of a society has a great bearing on the content of consciousness.

Every society, by its own practice of living and by the mode of relatedness, of feeling, and perceiving, develops a system of categories which determines the forms of awareness. This system works, as it were, like a *socially conditioned filter;* experience cannot enter awareness unless it can penetrate this filter.[15]

This "social filter," in Fromm's analysis, has three components: the language of the society, the form of logic which it assumes to be valid, and the taboos which the society enforces. Each of these components has its effect in filtering out, or excluding from awareness, certain types of experience, and giving prominence to other types. Since both language and logic are the products of a particular society, the third factor, the influence of the "social premium" placed on some experiences and the taboo placed on others, becomes predominant in Fromm's analysis.

Fromm elaborates upon the concept of social premium and social taboo in his analysis of the "social character." The social character is the means by which a society instills in its members a desire to preserve the patterns of life of that culture. If individuals are to desire to act as they must in a particular society, then thoughts and experiences which run counter to this functioning must be prevented. Not only is the individual forbidden to act on these impulses, in most cases they cannot even be allowed to enter his conscious awareness. Such thoughts and experiences must be repressed. "The individual cannot permit

15. *Ibid.,* p. 99. This passage suggests a kind of social determinism which seems to contradict Fromm's concept of individual "productivity."

himself to be aware of thoughts or feelings which are incompatible with the patterns of his culture, and hence he is forced to repress them." [16] To defy the culture is to run the risk of isolation and ostracism, a situation which for most men is unbearable.

Not only is consciousness *restricted* by social taboo; it is also *distorted* and *falsified* by a society which cannot allow the full realization of human potentiality. With regard to the extent of falsification, Fromm states: "The average person's consciousness is mainly 'false consciousness,' consisting of fictions and illusions, while precisely what he is not aware of is reality." [17]

Thus Fromm concludes that the content of consciousness is in large measure socially determined. Much, therefore, depends upon the extent to which the society encourages "full" awareness, the extent to which the "social aims" coincide with the "human aims." A society which fosters regressive answers to the human situation will force individuals to repress impulses which would lead them toward the fulfillment of the goal of human nature.

We have discussed three aspects of the process of achieving self-awareness: the development of intellection, the overcoming of narcissism, and the influence of society on the content of consciousness. It would seem that the first two lead necessarily to at least a temporary alienation; together they compose the basis for viewing oneself as a separate individual. The third factor, on the other hand, does not necessarily lead to alienation; in the "sane society," no artificial restrictions or falsifications would be imposed upon human consciousness. In actual societies, however, the experience which is allowed to pass through the "social filter" is a limited segment of the totality of possible human feeling and experience. Whereas the first two factors necessarily lead to a sense of separation and aloneness, the "social character" of a particular society may tend to accentuate

16. *Ibid.*, pp. 105–106.
17. *Ibid.*, p. 108.

this feeling, or to diminish it, depending upon whether the tone of the society is regressive or progressive. On the other hand, regressive tendencies within an individual may counteract progressive social tendencies, retarding the elimination of narcissism or regression.

In any case, the maturing individual must go through a stage of alienation: the separation of a limited consciousness from the whole man, which, we have seen, Fromm identifies with unconsciousness.

Inasmuch as consciousness represents only the small sector of socially patterned experience and unconsciousness represents the richness and depth of universal man the state of repressedness results in the fact that I, the accidental, social person, am separated from me the whole human person. I am a stranger to myself, and to the same degree everybody else is a stranger to me. I am cut off from the vast area of experience which is human, and remain a fragment of a man, a cripple who experiences only a small part of what is real in him and what is real in others.[18]

The individual who is "cut off from the vast area of experience which is human" cannot live productively. The alienated person is separated from his own powers. He does not experience himself as an active, creative center.

Let us summarize the results of our discussion. For Fromm, alienation is awareness of oneself as a separate being, in both the intellective and the affective senses—an awareness which has gone beyond the child's immediacy of experience but has not yet reached that fullness which sees man as he truly is, rooted in and harmoniously related to the cosmos. The overcoming of narcissism and the achievement of the "subject-object split" are necessary, though painful, forms of separation. In the stage of alienation, the awareness of separation tends to mask one's potentiality for a new relatedness through love, reason, and creative work. But the negative aspects of separation are overcome (without eliminating the separation) through the achievement of full consciousness.

18. *Ibid.,* p. 108.

Fromm applies this analysis both to the individual and to the human species. This means that alienation must be approached on two levels. In one sense, any physically mature person who has not achieved full consciousness is alienated. However, at the earlier stages of human evolution the objective conditions did not permit the achievement of the "sane society" or the realization of productive individuals in significant numbers. Speaking of all humanity, these stages represent infancy and adolescence and cannot be considered alienation in the fullest sense. In modern society, conditions permit the achievement of full consciousness and the sane society; yet they have not in fact been realized. Here is alienation in its most pernicious form, and it is this modern situation with which Fromm is primarily concerned.

The Question of Self-estrangement

A detailed critique of Fromm's view of alienation will be attempted in Chapter Nine from the theological point of view of Paul Tillich, employing the criterion of self-estrangement. Certain general comments might be made at this point. First, we conclude that for Fromm alienation and reconciliation are movements within nature. Though at one point Fromm speaks of man as "fallen out of nature," in his general perspective human potentialities are at the same time natural potentialities. Man transcends nature in order to fulfill and elevate nature, to "humanize" it. Human nature is one of nature's potentialities; it is derived from nature and therefore ultimately can be reconciled with it.

Second, human individuality and self-awareness, essential aspects of human nature, arise from the primal harmonies only through alienation. This means that alienation is a progressive, evolutionary step within nature, a necessary step toward the fulfillment of man (and thus of nature itself). Alienation is an aspect of the separation of man through self-consciousness from the primal harmonies.

Certain questionable consequences derive from this position. One consequence is that individuality and alienation appear to be, if not identical, at least interdependent in Fromm's account. But how then is individuality to be preserved when alienation is overcome? Fromm indeed affirms that man, through productivity, can be reunited with nature and himself without eliminating individuality. But this means that alienation and separation through self-awareness are not necessarily connected, that alienation somehow is a distortion of conscious separation. To use the philosophical terminology, there must be an essential separation (or individuality) as well as an existentially distorted separation. Fromm does not adequately preserve this distinction.

By the same token, Fromm's account through associating alienation with separation, fails to recognize that modes of separation and modes of union are interrelated. An individual in an alienated condition may submerge himself in some collectivity and still remain alienated. Distorted forms of separation and distorted forms of reunion are inseparable. Fromm sees that healthy self-consciousness is inseparable from healthy reunion, but he does not find this same interdependence in the alienated condition.

These lines of criticism suggest a critique of Fromm's understanding of the total self and its unity. It may be argued that the self is always individual *and* participant, even in its alienation. It reaches deeply into nature as well as emerging out of it. If its participation in various levels of reality, as well as its separation and individuality, may become alienated, then perhaps we have to do with a deeper alienation than Fromm acknowledges. If man's total being is alienated (if he is self-estranged), then nature, as well as man, will be affected. This at least is the Tillichian line of thought which we shall develop in Chapter Nine.

introductory survey of tillich's system: part one

The Relation of
Theology and Philosophy

P AUL TILLICH was born in Starzeddel, Germany, in 1886. He received his education at the universities of Berlin, Halle, and Breslau. He occupied chairs of theology and of philosophy in several German universities before being forced to leave Germany in 1933 because of his opposition of Nazism. Coming to the United States, he became Professor of Philosophical Theology at Union Theological Seminary and Columbia University, and, in 1955, University Professor at Harvard University. Since 1962 he has been John Nuveen Professor of Theology at the Divinity School of the University of Chicago.[1]

Since the beginning of his career, Tillich's primary identification has been as a philosophical theologian. His theological system is a philosophical theology in the classical sense of the term. A recent article introducing Tillich to French readers speaks of him as a philosophical theologian in the tradition of Augustine and Thomas Aquinas, venturing the opinion that he is perhaps the greatest theologian of this type that Protestantism has produced.[2] D. D. Williams suggests that the "weaving together of

1. For other biographical data see *Religion and Culture: Essays in Honor of Paul Tillich,* ed. by Walter Leibrecht.
2. Jean-Paul Gabus, "Un Grand Theologien: Paul Tillich," *Foi et Vie,* No. 6 (Nov.-Dec., 1960), p. 436.

theology and philosophy is the key to Tillich's method." [3]

In his willingness to bring philosophical concepts into the center of his theological system, Tillich can be distinguished from two major currents in modern Protestant theology on the basic question of theological method. On the one hand, liberal Protestant theology has tended to focus upon "religious experience" to the exclusion of "metaphysical speculations." This tendency is evident in the thought of Friedrich Schleiermacher and has characterized the liberal movement since his time. Albrecht Ritschl's appeal to moral rather than mystical experience did not fundamentally change this orientation. American "pragmatic empiricism" in theology continues this emphasis.

Tillich's theology deals extensively with human experience, as we shall see; but Tillich maintains that experience is the medium, and not the content, of religious truth. He rejects altogether the effort of some liberal theologians to employ the methods of experimental science in theology. This type of experience, where detachment is necessary, must be distinguished from mystical experience, or "experience by participation," which, according to Tillich, has a much more positive relation to theology. The experience of that which is "unconditional," of that which "concerns us ultimately," of "the holy," of that "which transcends the cleavage between subjectivity and objectivity" is fundamental to Tillich's whole system. But Tillich persists in the view that human experience as such cannot be the object of theology. Rather the object of theology is that which produces the experience. "The object of theology is what concerns us ultimately." [4] This is to say, its object is not the experience of ultimate concern as such.

This view of the object of theology leads Tillich, as we have suggested, to understand religious experience as a medium of religious truth, rather than its content. It further leads him to focus upon the category of "revelation" rather than religious

3. Daniel Day Williams, *What Present-Day Theologians Are Thinking*, p. 53.
4. Tillich, *Systematic Theology*, I, p. 12.

experience, though the latter may be the medium of revelation. The term revelation indicates to Tillich that the object of ultimate concern comes to experience rather than being derived from it. It produces the experience but is not contained in the experience.

The assertion of the centrality of revelation, while distinguishing Tillich's thought from the characteristic emphasis of liberalism, would seem to align him with the reaction against liberalism, known as "Neo-orthodox" or "Neo-Reformation" theology. This movement has made revelation the central category of religious truth and, like Tillich, has sharply differentiated theology from any form of empirical science. This theology, however, rejects not only an empirical theology in any form; it also seeks, as does liberalism, to exclude metaphysics in any form from the theological effort. Though there are diversities within the movement, the view of the Swedish theologian Gustaf Aulén may be taken as representative. In his systematic treatise, *The Faith of the Christian Church,* he states:

It is of utmost importance that a clear distinction be made between the affirmations of faith and rational metaphysics. Faith and its affirmations are one thing, metaphysics is something entirely different. That the differences are kept clearly in mind implies that the affirmations of faith are of a different nature than metaphysical theses, and that no combination of the theses of faith and metaphysics can be allowed.[5]

Aulén's comment that the Kantian "epistemological criticism of metaphysics" has "accomplished a liberation of systematic theology" might be taken as an attitude typical of the Neo-Reformation theology.[6]

Thus, although Tillich shares the emphasis upon revelation of the Neo-Reformation theology, he differs with this movement

5. Gustaf Aulén, *The Faith of the Christian Church,* p. 95; Emil Brunner's position consists of a strong affirmation of the primacy of the personal Biblical categories over the metaphysical categories.
6. *Ibid.,* p. 14.

as well as with liberalism in his approach to philosophical theology. Tillich shares his basic affirmation with Augustine and the Scholastics against liberalism and Neo-orthodoxy: the identification of the religious and the philosophical absolutes.

The religious and the philosophical Absolutes, *Deus* and *esse* cannot be unconnected! What is their connection from the point of view of being as well as of knowing? In the simple statement "God *is*," the connection is achieved; but the character of this connection is *the* problem in all problems of the philosophy of religion.[7]

The concept of being, or being-itself, is a philosophical concept (though, as we shall see, for Tillich it is derived from religious experience); but according to Tillich its use is necessary, not only in the philosophy of religion, but in systematic theology as well.

When a doctrine of God is initiated by defining God as being-itself, the philosophical concept of being is introduced into systematic theology. This was so in the earliest period of Christian theology and has been so in the whole history of Christian thought.[8]

Indeed, the assertion that God is being-itself is, for Tillich, the only nonsymbolic statement which can be made about God.[9]

The identification of *Deus* and *esse* means to Tillich that the ultimate object of theology and the ultimate object of metaphysics (Tillich prefers the term "ontology") are the same. Although the crucial question remains that of the actual relation between the two disciplines, the conclusion can already be drawn that there must be some positive relationship. It would seem apparent that Tillich in this primary assertion is very far from Aulén's view that "faith has really nothing to do with metaphysics." The difference between Tillich and Aulén (and

7. Tillich, "The Two Types of Philosophy of Religion," in *Theology of Culture*, p. 12.
8. Tillich, *Systematic Theology*, II, p. 10.
9. Tillich, *Systematic Theology*, I, pp. 238–239; cf. *Systematic Theology*, II, p. 10, where Tillich speaks of the term as the point at which "the symbolic and the non-symbolic coincide."

others of his persausion) is indeed great. However, the nature of this difference must not be prematurely oversimplified. When Tillich discusses the relationship of ontology and theology, he indicates (as we shall see) that they are independent but interrelated (the view to which Aulén and others object). Until the content which Tillich gives to the concept of being-itself has been fully explicated, however, his true understanding of the nature of ontology and its relation to theology remains obscured. The question of whether Tillich imports a "foreign metaphysic" into Christian theology, whether he allows Christian thought to be absorbed into an alien ontology, or whether he preserves a genuine independence and interrelation of the two disciplines cannot be answered until the function of being-itself in his system has been thoroughly explored.

Our first task must be a summary of Tillich's stated position on the question of the relation between ontology and theology. This analysis will be primarily derived from *Systematic Theology,* Vol. I, where Tillich has carefully elaborated his position. How is philosophical knowledge of being related to theological knowledge of God? As we have suggested, Tillich views the two ways of conceiving the ultimate as interdependent.

This means that the secular ultimates (the ontological concepts) and the sacred ultimates (the conceptions of God) are interdependent. Every ontological concept has a typical manifestation of man's ultimate concern in its background, although now it has been transformed into a definite concept. And every conception of God discloses special ontological assumptions in the categorical material it uses.[10]

On the one hand, then, Tillich traces the roots of certain important philosophical positions on the nature of being to their sources in "existential visions of what concerns man ultimately." [11] Similarly, he suggests that "a theological element, an ulti-

10. *Ibid.,* p. 221.
11. *Ibid.,* p. 230.

mate concern, gives the impulse to philosophy." [12] Thus every constructive philosopher is at the same time a theologian.

On the other hand, theology presupposes a developed ontology. Being cannot be described without the ontological categories.

We have searched for the object or question of theology, and we have discovered that a philosophical element is implied in theology —the question of the meaning and structure of being and its manifestation in the different realms of being.[13]

Tillich explicitly prefers ontological terms and categories for describing God to the personalistic terms and categories.

In spite of this interdependence, however, ontology and theology cannot be synthesized, in Tillich's view. Their independence is essentially based upon differences in perspective. These perspectives might be generally identified as the objective or detached and the "existential." This distinction is not absolute; theology must in part be objective and ontology must in part be existential. But they are to be distinguished by the dominant trend in each.

A slightly different formulation is suggested when Tillich indicates that theology is concerned with the power of being as contrasted with its structure. The object of theology

must be the Ground of our being, that which determines our being or not-being, the ultimate and unconditional power of being. But the power of being, its infinite ground or "being-itself," expresses itself in and through the structure of being.[14]

Considering Tillich's thought as a whole, it would seem (according to our analysis) that the choice here of the term "power of being" would be more appropriate than the somewhat more restricted phrase "the meaning of being for us" as the focal point of theology. We shall seek to show that the concept of the power

12. Tillich, *The Protestant Era,* p. 99.
13. *Ibid.*
14. Tillich, *Systematic Theology,* I, p. 21.

of being is central to Tillich's analysis of being. However, the investigation of the power of being may appear to be less existential; and indeed Tillich elsewhere concedes that it is a legitimate object of philosophy. "From Plato and Aristotle on, the concept of power plays an important role in ontological thought." [15] Perhaps for this reason Tillich on other occasions uses the term the "meaning of being," but the loss of meaning is only one of the threats to man which is overcome by the power of being. This difficulty in terminology already reflects a thoroughgoing difficulty in Tillich's thought which we shall seek to elucidate: the problem of making a genuinely fundamental distinction between ontology and theology.

Tillich's affirmation of the identity of the theological and ontological Absolutes, along with the asserted difference in perspective between the two fields, gives him a basis for his "method of correlation." Our understanding of this basis is not complete, however, without a survey of certain further assertions by Tillich concerning the actual content of ontology. First of all, Tillich can be said to accept the Kantian critique of speculative metaphysics, but only insofar as it is interpreted as the establishment of the finitude of human reason.

Finitude is essential for reason, as it is for everything that participates in being. The structure of this finitude is described in the most profound and comprehensive way in Kant's "critiques." The categories of experience are categories of finitude.[16]

The "finitude of reason" means to Tillich that reason cannot rise to knowledge of being-itself, that it cannot establish the existence of God through rational proofs. Here he does in fact agree with Kant; but Tillich departs from the explicit position of Kant in maintaining, as we shall see, that an essentialist ontology of finitude is possible. Tillich follows Martin Heidegger's interpretation of Kant's philosophy as at least implicitly

15. Tillich, *The Courage to Be,* p. 26.
16. Tillich, *Systematic Theology,* I, pp. 81–82.

containing the attempt to formulate an ontology of the structures of finitude as experienced by man in himself.[17]

It is not Tillich's intention, however, to subscribe to any particular metaphysical formulation, whether Kantian or existentialist. He seeks rather to appeal to the cumulative results of ontological reflection in the Western tradition. This becomes clear in his effort to define philosophy.

The suggestion made here is to call philosophy *that cognitive approach to reality in which reality as such is the object*. . . . Inquiring into the nature of reality as such means inquiring into those structures, categories, and concepts which are presupposed in the cognitive encounter with every realm of reality. From this point of view philosophy is by definition critical. It separates the multifarious materials of experience from those structures which make experience possible. There is no difference in this respect between constructive idealism and empirical realism.[18]

From this perspective Tillich criticizes both the system-builders, whose structures of thought are always disrupted by further gains in knowledge, and the logical positivists, who fail to see that all philosophy has ontological assumptions. The "general principles," the analysis of the structures of experience, remain as the legacy of philosophy through the centuries.

Only the general principles were left, always discussed, questioned, changed, but never destroyed, shining through the centuries, reinterpreted by every generation, inexhaustible, never antiquated or obsolete. These principles are the material of philosophy.[19]

17. Cf. Tillich, "Existential Philosophy: Its Historical Meaning," in *Theology of Culture*, pp. 97–98. Tillich's view of ontology appears to have been influenced at this point by Heidegger's study, *Kant and the Problem of Metaphysics*. Cf. Heidegger's statement of purpose: "the task of the following investigation is to explicate Kant's *Critique of Pure Reason* as a laying of the foundation of metaphysics in order thus to present the problem of metaphysics as the problem of a fundamental ontology.

"By fundamental ontology is meant that ontological analytic of man's finite essence which should prepare the foundation for the metaphysics 'which belongs to human nature.'" pp. 3–4.

18. Tillich, *Systematic Theology*, I, pp. 18–19.

19. *Ibid.*, p. 19.

This kind of summation of the assured results of ontological analysis is essential if Tillich's method of correlation is to be effective. If the ontological analysis of finite being is to raise the "question of God," it must be agreed on its "general principles." The theologian indeed must organize the ontological concepts, and view them "from the point of view of their theological significance." In doing so he may affect the analysis indirectly. But theology cannot organize the concepts of ontology if there are no such concepts generally agreed upon. Tillich, in fact, seems to see an ontological tradition possessing considerable continuity extending from the pre-Socratics to the present. It is significant to note that for Tillich the "philosophers of life" and the existentialists are representatives of this tradition in the modern period.[20] But it would not be correct, strictly speaking, to call Tillich's ontology an existentialist ontology, at least according to his own intention. He views it as a legitimate, though theologically oriented, summation of ontological reflection, including certain themes from existentialism.

Further Characteristics of Ontology

Certain further characteristics of ontology as Tillich understands it can now be described. First, ontology is the analysis of essential being, or what finitude is essentially, or the characteristics of finite being as such. This is what was meant in an earlier reference to the "structures, categories, and concepts which are presupposed in the cognitive encounter with every realm of reality." These elements are everywhere present, necessarily present, in every cognitive experience of reality. But something more than this is implied. Tillich, unlike Kant, holds that ontological reasoning can grasp the essences of real beings, that there is an exact correspondence between these structures of the

20. Cf. *ibid.,* p. 168. This understanding of these two philosophies as ontology can become a source of confusion in interpreting Tillich's system, for they both figure prominently in the analysis of human existence, which is to be distinguished in Tillich's thought from the ontological analysis now under discussion.

mind's cognitive encounter and the structures of the beings themselves. This assumption is based upon the affirmation that the "rational structure of the mind" corresponds to the "rational structure of reality." Tillich maintains that some form of correspondence between "subjective reason" and "objective reason" has been assumed throughout the philosophical tradition which we have been describing.

From the time of Parmenides it has been a common assumption of all philosophers that the *logos*, the word which grasps and shapes reality, can do so only because reality itself has a *logos* character. There have been widely differing explanations of the relation between the *logos* structure of the grasping-and-shaping-self and the *logos* structure of the grasped-and-shaped-world. But the necessity of an explanation has been acknowledged almost unanimously.[21]

Theology, according to Tillich, is not committed to any of the specific ways in which this relationship is described. The correspondence is affirmed theologically, however, in the form of the doctrine of the "image of God." Tillich takes the image of God in man to be man's rationality, the fact that man's *logos* corresponds to the *logos* of creation.

Man is the image of God in that in which he differs from all other creatures, namely, his rational structure. . . . Man is the image of God because his *logos* is analogous to the divine *logos*.[22]

Ultimately, Tillich's position here seems to be an ontological assertion: nothing can be completely strange to man, since all beings share in the structure of finitude which man experiences in himself, the structure of the "self-world correlation," or self-relatedness.

Since everything that is participates in the self-world structure of being, elements of self-relatedness are universal. This makes [cognitive] union with everything possible. Nothing is absolutely strange.[23]

21. *Ibid.*, p. 75.
22. *Ibid.*, p. 259.
23. *Ibid.*, p. 97. Tillich's concept of self-relatedness as the basic structure of being will be the subject of further discussion throughout this

Essential reason, then, knows the essences of things, and all beings, like reason itself, are essentially finite.

Ontology might be said, then, to have as its object the description of essential finitude, and essential reason might be said to be equipped for this task. However, these judgments must be qualified. It is true for Tillich that essential reason is competent to deal with essential finitude. But this assertion raises the question of the meaning of the term "essential" here. Actual reason, like actual finite existence, is "fallen," estranged from its essence. Therefore, as we shall see in more detail, the full understanding of essential reason and essential finitude belongs to the theological "answer." Our analysis of essential finitude might be anticipated here by indicating that for Tillich essential finitude is finitude-in-unity-with-being-itself. Likewise, essential reason is reason-in-unity-with-being-itself.

The implications of this for finitude will be discussed below. For reason this means that essentially there is a "depth of reason" which shines through each of its acts without being conceptualized in any. Thus, although reason cannot grasp being-itself, it is essentially related to being-itself. This formulation enables Tillich to maintain that revelation does not destroy reason but fulfills it. In actual reason, then, this depth appears primarily as a question, rather than a reality. Actual ontology in its analysis of finitude must raise the question of being-itself. Finitude taken alone is not self-explanatory; it is a question rather than an answer.

This view of finitude brings to the fore a second characteristic of ontology as Tillich understands it. The question arises: what is the nature of actual ontological reflection concerning the reality of the ontological Absolute, or being-itself? Tillich's answer might be summarized as follows: ontology presupposes the presence of an "unconditional element in the structure of

---

study. Tillich's epistemology cannot be treated adequately apart from his ontology. His concept of reason cannot be understood apart from the ontological realities of freedom and self-transcendence, which we shall examine.

reason and reality," but it cannot establish the existence of an unconditioned being.

This position taken by Tillich might be explained by indicating that he accepts the ontological argument of Augustine and Anselm, not as a proof for the existence of a Supreme Being, but as establishing that the reality of truth-itself is assumed by any assertion of truth.

> *Veritas* is presupposed in every philosophical argument; and *veritas* is God. You cannot deny truth as such because you could do it only in the name of truth, thus establishing truth. And if you establish truth you affirm God.[24]

There would seem to be two somewhat different aspects to Tillich's concept of the unconditional: the cognitive and the religious (these, as we shall see, are interrelated). Concerning the cognitive aspect, Tillich holds that the unconditional element transcends the subject-object relation, and therefore represents a point of "identity."

> The Anselmian statement that God is a necessary thought and that therefore this idea must have objective as well as subjective reality is valid in so far as thinking, by its very nature, implies an unconditional element which transcends subjectivity and objectivity, that is, a point of identity which makes the idea of truth possible.[25]

This unconditional element is present in both the subjective and the objective structures of reason but transcends them both. Nothing is more fundamental to Tillich's thought than the idea that being-itself transcends the subject-object relation, and therefore transcends reason.

It is equally significant for the cognitive aspect of ontology, however, that the unconditional must be assumed—that there is "a point of identity which makes the idea of truth possible." Ontology presupposes the unconditional in this sense; but it cannot, by its examination of being, establish the existence of

24. Tillich, "The Two Types of Philosophy of Religion," in *Theology of Culture*, p. 12.
25. Tillich, *Systematic Theology*, I, p. 207.

anything which is unconditioned. Being is finite and conditioned. Thus ontology raises the question of the unconditional, of being-itself, but cannot answer the question.

Since the interest of ontology in being is mainly theoretical or cognitive, the question of truth is its dominant interest. There is, however, another aspect of the unconditional, which we have called the religious aspect, which ontology cannot avoid, though this aspect is not its dominant interest. The awareness of the unconditional, according to Tillich, is not a merely cognitive apprehension. To be aware of the unconditioned means to be conditioned by it with one's whole being.

Awareness of the unconditional is itself unconditional, and there-fore beyond the division of psychological functions. It was a main interest of Augustinian psychology to show the mutual immanence of the functions of the soul and the impossibility of separating them in their relation to the *esse, verum, bonum*. It is impossible to be aware of the Unconditioned as if it did not exclude by its very pres-ence any observer who was not conditioned by it in his whole being.[26]

This means that the unconditioned which is apprehended as the basis of truth is also apprehended as the basis or ground of being, and the ground of goodness. Man as a whole being is aware of the unconditioned; in this sense the awareness is "existential," and to this extent we may say that ontology is based upon an existential apprehension. Thus, the awareness of the uncondi-tioned is the foundation upon which both ontology and theology are built, though their interests in relation to it differ.

This existential root of ontology has important implications. The philosopher asks the question of the unconditional by virtue of his very existence as a human being. But he asks this question, according to Tillich, as the result of an apprehension of something unconditional, an "ultimate concern." The philoso-pher, "like every human being, . . . exists in the power of an

26. Tillich, "The Two Types of Philosophy of Religion," in *Theology of Culture,* p. 23.

ultimate concern, whether or not he is fully conscious of it, whether or not he admits it to himself and to others."[27] The question which the philosopher asks about being-itself is actually, then, the result of a prior "answer," a concrete apprehension of the unconditional. Thus the formulation of the question of God or being-itself is not simply autonomous and secular ontological analysis. It is a response to a "revelation," however fragmentary, of being-itself. This means that the ontological question, formulated under the impact of some "answer," some manifestation of being-itself, can legitimately be "correlated" with the Christian theological answer. It further means that the formulation of the question may be fragmentary, from a theological point of view, if the "revelation" were fragmentary. This would necessitate what we have called elsewhere the "elevation" of the question, as well as of the attempted ontological answer.

A third important characteristic of ontology remains to be described. According to Tillich, the only promising path to ontological understanding leads through man's own nature. This truth also he takes to be implicitly or explicitly acknowledged in the ontological tradition of which we have spoken.

Man occupies a pre-eminent position in ontology, not as an outstanding object among other objects, but as that being who asks the ontological question and in whose self-awareness the ontological answer can be found. The old tradition—expressed equally by mythology and mysticism, by poetry and metaphysics—that the principles which constitute the universe must be sought in man is indirectly and involuntarily confirmed, even by the behavioristic self-restriction. "Philosophers of life" and "Existentialists" have reminded us in our time of this truth on which ontology depends.[28]

As we commented earlier, this does not mean that Tillich would describe all ontology as existentialist. It means, on the contrary, that Tillich sees an element of essentialism in existentialist philosophy. He suggests here that the essential structures of finitude

27. Tillich, *Systematic Theology*, I, p. 24.
28. *Ibid.*, p. 168.

are available to man in the implicit structure of his own experience. This means that the "self-world polarity," which is the irreducible structure of man's experience, is "the basic articulation of being." Its analysis is the basic task of ontology.

The self having a world to which it belongs—this highly dialectical structure—logically and experientially precedes all other structures. Its analysis should be the first step in every ontological task.[29]

The meaning of this understanding of ontology will be a subject of consideration throughout our study of Tillich. From the perspective of this study the observation might be made (to be verified later) that the self-world polarity is, for Tillich, rooted in the ability of being, as life, to transcend itself. That a being can go out from itself indicates that there is a certain duality and self-relatedness in the being. The subject-object relation is simply the ultimate fulfillment of this possibility, which is inherent in all being.

A new difficulty arises for ontology when it is understood to derive its data from the structure of human experience. Man in his existence has become "estranged" from his essence. Tillich sees this fact as derived, not only from the Christian doctrine of the "fall," but also from the century-old existentialist analysis of man's predicament (not to speak of Plato and others in the ontological tradition). The nature of this estrangement will be analyzed in detail in the next chapter. Our concern here is with the implications of this estrangement for ontology. It is with the consideration of estrangement that the uniqueness of existentialism comes to the fore, as far as Tillich is concerned. It is existentialism (understood as a revolt against the premature reconciliation in Hegel's system) which makes the distinction between man's existence and his essence. This distinction is always implied in an existentialist analysis, although specific existentialists may deny the reality of man's essential nature.

For ontology, this distinction means two things. First, man's estranged existence may be confused by the ontologist with his

29. *Ibid.*, pp. 164–165.

essential finitude, thus suggesting the mistaken conclusion that man is essentially in a state of estrangement. Secondly, reason itself, as a part of man's existence, is estranged from its own essence. Reason shares the fate of being.

> Reason as the structure of mind and reality is actual in the processes of being, existence, and life. Being is finite, existence is self-contradictory, and life is ambiguous.... Actual reason participates in these characteristics of reality.[30]

Thus reason is not only limited to finitude and confined to raising the question of God; in its actualization in human life it is also disrupted, estranged from its own nature and from its source. It needs reconciliation.

Our conclusions concerning the content of actual ontology in Tillich's view might be summarized. First, the proper object of reason is finitude, and the legitimate aim of ontology is a description of the essential structures of finitude. However, finitude (even if its structures can be discerned apart from their existential distortion) is not comprehensible in and of itself; it is a puzzle for actual reason—for that reason which is severed from its own depth. But, in the second place, actual reason must assume what it cannot establish—the reality of the unconditioned, at least in the form of truth-itself. This assumption is not itself based upon reason, but upon an existential awareness. Finally, "the way to ontology leads through the nature of man." The structures of finitude are best approached through the study of the underlying structure of human experience, the self-world polarity. The attempt to reduce one pole to the other must fail. Since this is the case, ontology experiences another difficulty: not only are the structures of finitude not self-explanatory; in man they have become existentially distorted. Ontology, insofar as it is successful in distinguishing the structures of finitude from their existential distortion, raises the question of God or being-itself. It is the special task of existentialism to describe the separation of existence from these essential structures.

30. *Ibid.*, p. 81.

Ontology and Theology Correlated

These characteristics of ontology make possible a correlation between theology and ontology (as well as a correlation between theology and the analysis of existence). Both ontology and theology, as we have seen, are based upon an existential awareness, or revelation, of being-itself. This is the basis for the possibility of a positive relation between them. In its method, ontology seeks to minimize the effect of its existential or religious source and to describe in a detached fashion the universal structures of being. This effort partly succeeds; but ontology cannot explain how being, in its finitude, sustains itself. The quest for an unconditioned being fails.

Theology, on the other hand, seeks to explicate fully the concrete existential manifestation of being-itself which it has received. In order to display the universal and unconditioned character of being-itself, however, theology must inevitably employ ontological categories and rational structures. Further, in order for the theological answer to be relevant to the human situation, it must be presented as an answer to the question which ontology actually asks: the question of being and truth itself. Tillich views the ontological question as the fundamental question which man asks. Therefore, the theological answer must be given in an ontological form. God must be viewed first of all as being-itself, or the ground of being.

Thus, although the ultimate source for knowledge of God in Tillich's thought is revelation, the concept of God is formulated in ontological terms and categories. This fact has led various interpreters of Tillich to question whether the ontological factors in his concept overshadow the revelational or, more specifically, the Biblical categories of thought. This question is based upon an assumed contrast between the ontological concept of God as developed in the tradition of classical Greek metaphysics and the God of Old and New Testaments, the God of Abraham, Isaac, Jacob, and Jesus. The concept of being as it was developed in the thought of such men as Parmenides, Plato, and Plotinus was a largely static concept. In the words of Charles Hartshorne, the deity of Greek metaphysics was thought of as "an absolute, infinite, immutable, simple, impassive deity."[31] This view, on the face of it, stands in sharp contrast to the dynamic concept of Yahweh, the Lord of history, found in the Bible. Can the two be reconciled? Tillich's answer to this problem is the subject of our next chapter.

31. Charles Hartshorne, *The Divine Relativity,* p. 26.

introductory
survey of
tillich's system:
part two

God as the Power of Being W E MUST now ask:
how does Tillich deal with this tension between Greek metaphysics and Biblical revelation? If the concept of being-itself is the basis for thought about God, are the Biblical characteristics superimposed upon a foundation which is fundamentally alien to them? W. M. Horton identifies the main unresolved issue concerning the nature of God in contemporary theology as "the question whether the Greek metaphysical conception of God as Absolute Being can really be reconciled with the Biblical conception of God as the Almighty Father and Creator." In discussing Tillich's position, Horton suggests that for Tillich the Greek conception (presumably the static conception described above) is primary. "Tillich begins with the ontological element in the concept of God, and then adds the Biblical attributes of holiness, love, and power, as Thomas Aquinas does."[1]

If, as many believe, Tillich's formulation of the doctrine of God can be accurately described in this fashion, it can be criticized from various perspectives within Protestantism. Thus, Aulén speaks of the inevitable spirit of compromise which characterizes all scholastic theology. Nels Ferré voices a criticism

1. Horton, *Christian Theology: An Ecumenical Approach*, p. 96.

which others might well share: if one starts with the concept of being, the dynamism of Biblical thought is lost. "Start with being as ultimate, and arrive at no adequate doctrine of becoming."[2] The judgment that Tillich begins with a static concept of being, however, must be challenged. This requires a close examination of Tillich's concept of being-itself.

We shall seek to establish that a dynamic concept is at the heart of Tillich's formulation of being-itself: the concept of "life." If our attempt succeeds, we can say that Tillich's formulation represents a victory of the "living God" of the Scriptures over the Greek Absolute. The victory is only partial, however; Tillich's concept of life is itself built upon the Greek categories of being and nonbeing.

The dynamism in Tillich's concept of God is partially disguised by the term being-itself, a term which for many has static implications. It is more fully revealed in a phrase which Tillich associates most closely with being-itself: the "power of being." At times, Tillich seeks to preserve a distinction between the two by suggesting that while being-itself is a nonsymbolic concept, the "power of being" is metaphorical. Thus in *Love, Power, and Justice* he states:

What can we say fundamentally about the nature of being? . . . Nothing in terms of definition, but something in terms of metaphorical indication. And we suggested the concept of power for this purpose: Being is the power of being![3]

Elsewhere, however, Tillich fails to preserve this distinction. In his systematic discussion of "God as Being," Tillich states:

The concept of being as being, or being-itself, points to the power inherent in everything, the power of resisting nonbeing. Therefore, instead of saying that God is first of all being-itself, it is possible to say that he is the power of being in everything and above everything, the infinite power of being.[4]

2. Nels F. S. Ferré, *The Christian Understanding of God*, p. 29.
3. Tillich, *Love, Power, and Justice*, p. 37.
4. Tillich, *Systematic Theology*, I, p. 236.

Tillich cites this meaning of the term being-itself as a defense
against the criticism that it is simply the "highest abstraction."

It is the expression of the experience of being over against nonbeing. Therefore, it can be described as the power of being which
resists nonbeing.

. . . .

God is being-itself, in the sense of the power of being or the power
to conquer nonbeing.[5]

It would seem that the power of being is what the term being-
itself *means* to Tillich; whenever the latter term is given content
it becomes the former. The point to Tillich's distinction apparently is that the term "power" is used symbolically when applied
to God. But if the only nonsymbolic term has no real content
until it becomes symbolic, Tillich has not really succeeded in
preserving the concept of being-itself as both meaningful and
nonsymbolic. Rather, his actual position seems to be that the
"power of being" is an effective symbol for the divine presence
and operation. This is what being-itself *means*.

When being-itself is viewed as the power of being, it becomes,
in Tillich's analysis, inseparable from a concept of nonbeing.
Indeed, the ontological question arises as the result of man's
recognition of the possibility of his own nonbeing. Tillich follows
Plato in distinguishing a nonbeing which is the "absolute negation of being," and a nonbeing which is "the relative negation
of being"; the latter can have a "dialectical" relation to being.
Tillich holds that in order to conceive of finite being the latter
concept is necessary.

If being and nothingness are placed in absolute contrast, nonbeing
is excluded from being in every respect; everything is excluded
except being-itself (i.e., the whole world is excluded). There can be
no world unless there is a dialectical participation of nonbeing in
being.[6]

Therefore it must be said, first of all, that finitude includes

5. Tillich, *Systematic Theology,* II, p. 11.
6. Tillich, *Systematic Theology,* I, p. 187.

the threat of nonbeing; it is within finitude, so to speak. "Non-being is the negation of being within being-itself. . . . Being which includes nonbeing is finite being. 'Finite' means carrying within one's being the destiny not to be."[7] As we have seen, the power of being within finitude is viewed as the power to resist nonbeing. Tillich further holds, however, that, speaking meta-phorically, being-itself must be viewed as eternally overcoming its own nonbeing.

If one is asked how nonbeing is related to being-itself, one can only answer metaphorically: being "embraces" itself and nonbeing. Being has nonbeing "within" itself as that which is eternally present and eternally overcome in the process of the divine life. The ground of everything that is, is not a dead identity without movement and becoming; it is living creativity. Creatively it affirms itself, eternally conquering its own nonbeing.[8]

Indeed, being cannot be thought without thinking its possible negation. It can be defined as the "negation of possible non-being."

This nonbeing within the divine being is explained elsewhere as the nonbeing of finitude which is overcome within the divine life.

God is infinite because he has the finite (and with it that element of nonbeing which belongs to finitude) within himself united with his infinity. One of the functions of the symbol "divine life" is to point to this situation.[9]

This means that insofar as finitude is "within" the divine life its negativity is overcome, but insofar as it is "outside" the divine life nonbeing remains as a threat. The dynamic element in God can be expressed as the negative element in the ground of being which is overcome as negative in the process of being-itself. As such it is the basis of the negative element in the creature, in which it is not overcome but is effective as a threat and a potential disruption.[10]

7. Tillich, *Love, Power, and Justice*, pp. 38–39.
8. Tillich, *The Courage to Be*, p. 34.
9. Tillich, *Systematic Theology*, I, p. 252.
10. *Ibid.*, pp. 246–247.

As has already been implied, it is the presence of a dialectical nonbeing in God which makes him the ground of life. It is this negativity which makes being dynamic. A dynamic understanding of reality

is possible only if one accepts the view that nonbeing belongs to being, that being could not be the Ground of life without nonbeing. ... Nonbeing drives being out of its seclusion, it forces it to affirm itself dynamically.[11]

That is to say, nonbeing forces being to transcend itself without limit, to go beyond itself creatively. This means that when Tillich speaks of God as being-itself he is not far from the affirmation of God as living, contrary to some theological criticism. Being-itself is the power of being to overcome nonbeing, and this power Tillich understands as a characteristic of life. It is the threat of nonbeing which forces being to affirm itself dynamically, that is, to transcend itself as life. It is appropriate then that in the *Systematic Theology* the discussion of "God as Being" is immediately followed by "God as Living."

The fact of Tillich's emphasis upon the dynamic nature of God's life is also partly obscured by his statement that life must be attributed to God symbolically rather than literally. Taken literally, life suggests incompleteness and contingency, characteristics which cannot be attributed to God. Tillich argues that the nonsymbolic description of God as "becoming" (in some process philosophies) suffers this limitation. These philosophies do not recognize that God's being is more basic than his becoming.

As the system develops, however, it becomes clear that Tillich's distinction is not so much between being and becoming as between "ambiguous" and "unambiguous" life. In the former, self-transcendence threatens the loss of self-identity; creativity may lead to a chaotic indeterminacy. But in the divine life "self-transcendence never is in tension with self-preservation."[12] In

11. Tillich, *The Courage to Be*, p. 179.
12. Tillich, *Systematic Theology*, I, p. 244.

going beyond himself, God does not cease to be God. Elsewhere, Tillich suggests that this balance characterizes life essentially.

> Every living being (and, in terms of analogy, every being) drives beyond itself and beyond the given form through which it has being. In man's essential nature dynamics and form are united. Even if a given form is transcended, this happens in terms of form.[13]

Again, he admits tensions, but not conflicts, into the unity of unambiguous life.

> The dynamics of all life, even the unambiguous life of the transcendent union, implies tensions. But only in the estrangement of ambiguous life do the tensions become conflicts.[14]

It would appear that Tillich's criticism of process philosophy and the "becoming" God is based upon this distinction of ambiguous and unambiguous life rather than upon the designation of God's life as "symbolic." A philosophy which fails to recognize the essential characteristics of life falsely attributes to God characteristics which belong to life only in existential distortion. After this distinction has been made, the characteristics of essential or unambiguous life can be attributed to being-itself. On the basis of this analysis it might be preferable to consider Tillich's basic assertion to be that God is unambiguous life (or eternal life), rather than being-itself. This latter term has caused Tillich's thought to be misunderstood.

Our analysis has shown that Tillich's concept of being-itself contains a dynamic element, the overcoming of nonbeing. We have further indicated his view that this dynamic element in being-itself is essential in order to understand God as the living God who is the ground of life. Beyond this, the analysis has shown that Tillich's rejection of the view of God as "becoming" does not necessitate a rejection of the symbol of the living God. If we are correct in viewing this symbol as central to Tillich's view of God, then Tillich in summarizing the proponents of this

13. Tillich, *Systematic Theology*, II, p. 64.
14. Tillich, *Systematic Theology*, III, p. 157.

view of God must give us a clue to the tradition in which he himself stands.

Philosophy has dealt with the dynamic self-affirmation of being-itself wherever it spoke dialetically, notably in Neoplatonism, Hegel, and the philosophers of life and process. Theology has done the same whenever it took the idea of the living God seriously, most obviously in the trinitarian symbolization of the inner life of God.[15]

It would seem fair to suggest that Tillich stands in this tradition. If so, it is not correct to associate him with those who import the concept of being in the static sense into the Christian tradition. Rather, we might say that his ontology reflects the influence of the dynamism of the Judeo-Christian concept of God. However, further clarification of his concept of life is necessary.

Further Analysis of the Concept of Life

One of the main goals of our whole analysis of Tillich is to indicate the richness of the concept of "life" in his system. Although the analysis of the ambiguities of life has its special place in the system in correlation with the Christian answer of "Spirit" or "unambiguous life" (vol. III, part IV), in fact the concept of life pervades Tillich's perspective in its entirety. In his systematic treatment of the concept in vol. III he suggests a relationship between his thought and that of certain philosophers of life or process (e.g., Nietzsche, Dilthey, Bergson, Whitehead). Elsewhere, however, he indicates that his approach to life is rooted in the earlier writings of Hegel, and we have found this relationship suggestive for our study.

In this introductory chapter we shall attempt to provide a synoptic overview of Tillich's system, showing the centrality of the concept of life both in his analysis of God and of his creatures. This general survey will provide a framework within which

15. Tillich, *The Courage to Be*, pp. 179–180. For the view of Tillich's ontology developed in this and the following section, cf. my article, "Tillich on the Personal God," *The Journal of Religion*, XLIV (October, 1964), pp. 289–293.

our analysis of estrangement in subsequent chapters can be comprehended.

Tillich calls his concept of life "dialectical." By this term he seems to mean the characteristic of life to go out from itself and return to itself.

In a dialectical description one element of a concept drives to another. Taken in this sense, dialectics determine all life-processes and must be applied in biology, psychology, and sociology. The description of tensions in living organisms, neurotic conflicts, and class struggles is dialectical. Life itself is dialectical. If applied symbolically to the divine life, God as a living God must be described in dialectical statements. He has the character of all life, namely, to go beyond himself and to return to himself.[16]

Elsewhere, Tillich emphasizes the element of negativity in the movement of life. In describing the dialectical method, Tillich states:

It presupposes that reality itself moves through "yes" and "no," through positive, negative, and positive again. The dialectical method attempts to mirror the movement of reality. It is the logical expression of a philosophy of life, for life moves through self-affirmation, going out of itself and returning to itself.[17]

When Tillich speaks of life as separating itself from itself and returning to itself, and of this separation as a form of negativity, he seems to refer to the movement of being in the face of non-being which we have described above. Tillich understands life also as "the actualization of potential being."[18] As such, life moves from the "already" into the "not yet." This is true of the divine life as well as of finite life. Describing the dynamic element in the divine life, Tillich states:

The divine creativity, God's participation in history, his outgoing character, are based on this dynamic element. It includes a "not yet"

16. Tillich, *Systematic Theology,* II, p. 90.
17. Tillich, *Systematic Theology,* I, p. 234. In *Systematic Theology,* III, p. 11, he observes that "the polarity of life and death has always colored the word 'life.' "
18. Tillich, *Systematic Theology,* III, p. 30.

which is, however, always balanced by an "already" within the divine life. It is not an absolute "not yet," which would make it a divine-demonic power, nor is the "already" an absolute already. It also can be expressed as the negative element in the ground of being which is overcome as negative in the process of being-itself.[19]

It is this "not yet" which is the element of nonbeing in the finitude which belongs to the divine life.

By the same token, life is necessarily creative. In actualizing its potentialities life creates itself. This is true of the divine life and, in a derivative sense, of finite life also. For Tillich, the divine life and the divine self-creativity are identical.[20] Likewise, Tillich considers the self-creation of finite life to be one of its basic functions.[21]

The power of life, finally, is the power of self-transcendence. This important concept is involved in every aspect of our problem and will be analyzed further in the next chapter. Tillich at one point seeks to preserve a distinction between that going out of itself which we have identified as the self-creativity of life and the function of self-transcendence as such. According to this distinction, creativity appears on the horizontal level, while self-transcendence suggests that function of life whereby it rises above itself vertically in the direction of the infinite.[22] Later, however, Tillich acknowledges that self-transcendence cannot be viewed as a separate function of life but must be understood as an aspect or quality of the other functions (in human life, self-integration or morality as well as self-creation or culture).[23] For our purposes, therefore, self-transcendence may be viewed as the most significant aspect of that going out of itself which constitutes life. It is to be found in all levels or "dimensions" of life but comes to its fullest realization in man. In its symbolic application to God, of course, there can be no distinction between horizontal and vertical directions.

19. Tillich, *Systematic Theology*, I, p. 246.
20. *Ibid.*, p. 252.
21. Cf. Tillich, *Systematic Theology*, III, pp. 30 ff.
22. *Ibid.*, p. 31.
23. *Ibid.*, pp. 96–97.

The power of self-transcendence can be identified as the power of being to overcome nonbeing. As we have seen, this power is the power of being-itself. When self-transcendence is found in finitude it indicates the presence of the power of being.

> The power of infinite self-transcendence is an expression of man's belonging to that which is beyond nonbeing, namely, to being-itself. The potential presence of the infinite (as unlimited self-transcendence) is the negation of the negative element in finitude. It is the negation of nonbeing.[24]

The presence of God is known through the power of life in the creature to drive beyond itself or transcend itself. Finite life gains its power to transcend itself, to overcome nonbeing, through participation in the life of God, the power of being.

We have already observed that Tillich applies the category of life both to the finite world and to the divine. We are now in a position to indicate his view of the relation between the divine life and finite life. We have just noted that finite self-transcendence is rooted in the power of being. Beyond this, however, we must conclude that for Tillich finite self-transcendence *is* the divine self-transcendence. The divine going beyond itself is fulfilled in the human going beyond itself.

This identity is indicated, for example, in Tillich's brief discussion of his concept of God as "self-transcendent." There he observes that "the divine transcendence is identical with the freedom of the created to turn away from the essential unity with the creative ground of its being." [25] We shall establish in the next chapter that self-transcendence and freedom are very closely related in Tillich's thought. If this is the case, then Tillich in identifying divine transcendence and human freedom is, in fact, equating divine and human self-transcendence. This means that the divine life completes its own self-transcendence by pouring itself creatively into an infinite variety of finite forms. In creating life, it gives to these forms the power of self-tran-

---

24. Tillich, *Systematic Theology,* I, p. 191.
25. Tillich, *Systematic Theology,* II, p. 8.

scendence, which reaches its fulfillment in human freedom. Only here does life (either human or divine) reach true or complete self-transcendence; for in the actualization of finite freedom, finitude moves "outside" the divine life. This transcendence of the divine life is achieved in the power of the divine life, although it is achieved through the instrumentality of human freedom.

This concept of the divine life and creativity "poured into" finitude, giving it the power of self-transcendence, forms the background for Tillich's treatment of the theological doctrines of "creation" and of "the fall." We might say here in anticipation of our detailed analysis that a certain degree of self-transcendence produces the possibility of finite freedom—provides its ontological basis. The appearance of freedom is the culmination of an ontological movement, the process of life achieving self-transcendence. But the *act* of realizing freedom is viewed by Tillich as a conscious human choice and thus not a "structural necessity." Conscious choice must accompany the achievement of a certain degree of self-separation.

We can now observe that life in self-transcendence produces the subject-object split and self-consciousness. Life develops self-separation to the point where self-awareness is reached. In Tillich's view, all beings are "self-related," all participate to some degree in the "self-world polarity." But in man, self-relatedness and self-transcendence come to fruition in self-consciousness (and hence in freedom). For Tillich, the subject-object division is "a decisive moment in the self-transcendence of life." [26] This is the case because it is at the point of the emergence of self-consciousness and freedom that Tillich visualizes life prepared to "go out" from the divine life in (partial) independence of the ground of being.

Let us now summarize Tillich's scheme as we have conceived it. The divine life and creativity reaches the point in man of going out from itself in full self-transcendence. Up to this point, separation within the divine life is balanced by reunion; but the

26. Tillich, *Systematic Theology*, III, p. 92.

completion of God's creation requires a free act, which is at the same time a creative act, on the part of man. The one continuous movement of the divine life in its creativity produces life which goes out beyond the divine life in self-consciousness and freedom. Man's free and creative act of self-transcendence is at the same time God's act of self-transcendence. The creation (outside the divine life) is, in a real sense, ontologically a part of the divine life (its own self-transcendence). At the same time, man and his world stand upon man's freedom in separation from the Ground.

We shall give a detailed exposition of these points in subsequent chapters. We might observe here that Tillich's concept of life contains the ideas of the overcoming of nonbeing, the movement from potentiality to actuality, creativity, self-transcendence, freedom, and self-consciousness. Surely a concept with this richness of implication is a key to much of Tillich's system and cannot be ignored in any exposition of its main themes. It would appear that many of the critical appraisals of Tillich's thought have overlooked the centrality of this conception.

Our analysis is incomplete, however, for Tillich further conceives life to be "ambiguous." In his explicit account, ambiguity appears where there is a mixture of essential and existential elements. "Life always includes essential and existential elements; this is the root of its ambiguity." [27] However, this formulation is inadequate as an explanation of the meaning of ambiguity. Tillich can say elsewhere that fulfillment of the creature depends upon a "creative synthesis" of essence and existence.[28]

It would appear that Tillich's conception can better be understood in terms of the process of self-transcendence. At one point he observes that self-transcendence is two-sided: an expression of the power of being and a separation from its source. "The process of self-transcendence carries a double meaning in each

27. *Ibid.*, p. 107.
28. *Ibid.*, p. 401; elsewhere he speaks of the "reunion of essence and existence" as the final aim of reality.

of its moments. At one and the same time it is an increase and a decrease in the power of being." [29] Again, Tillich observes somewhat cryptically that "in every act of human creativity the element of separation from the creative ground is effective. Human creation is ambiguous." [30] In these statements as elsewhere Tillich is suggesting that the basic movement of life contains both a positive and a negative aspect. This means, in effect, that life is tragic. It becomes separated from its source and ground by its own greatness, its own self-transcendence and creativity. Thus Tillich states:

> The self-transcendence of life, which reveals itself to man as the greatness of life, leads under the conditions of existence to the tragic character of life, to the ambiguity of the great and the tragic. [31]

One might speculate as to Tillich's basic intuition here. Could it be that he is most impressed with the tragic quality of human creativity? In his own account of creativity a paradoxical quality can be seen. On the one hand, in the *eschaton* human creativity and divine revelation will be one. "Man's creativity and divine self-manifestation are one in the fulfilled Kingdom of God." [32] On the other hand, one of the primary marks of sin is the fact that "man identifies his cultural creativity with divine creativity." [33] In Tillich's account, human greatness drives toward *hubris,* especially in great men. Clearly, for Tillich, it is not the type of creativity but creativity as such which is tragic. Thus it is self-transcendence as creativity which enters most directly into Tillich's concept of sin and estrangement.

The understanding of life as tragic must be distinguished from the view that finitude as such is tragic. Tillich denies that the latter is the case, for finitude may exist in unity with its Ground. But life is ambiguous and, it would appear, tragic as well in its

29. Tillich, *Systematic Theology,* I, p. 190.
30. *Ibid.,* p. 256.
31. Tillich, *Systematic Theology,* III, p. 92.
32. *Ibid.,* p. 403.
33. Tillich, *Systematic Theology,* II, p. 51.

inherent going-beyond-itself. Its greatness is at the same time its weakness.

This is not to say that life cannot be "elevated beyond itself," cannot be saved. What has been said thus far refers to what Tillich calls "the natural form of man's self-transcendence." It is ambiguous, tragic; it "remains a question." The main purpose of our analysis in the following chapters is to describe the negative aspects of this separation, which Tillich calls estrangement. We must observe at this point, however, that Tillich employs the concept of self-transcendence in a different sense in his analysis of reconciliation. It will serve our summary purposes to describe some aspects of Tillich's view of reconciliation at this point before turning to a detailed account of estrangement.

Reconciliation as Ecstatic Self-Transcendence

In his elaboration of the concept of unambiguous life, Tillich speaks of finite life elevated by the Divine Spirit into "a successful self-transcendence." This idea is identical with the concept of "ecstasy" which appears in various parts of Tillich's system. And it is notable that love as successful reunion is viewed as ecstatic in this same sense. It is clear that Tillich is speaking in these areas of another form of self-transcendence.

The two forms of self-transcendence would appear to be distinguished most significantly by their relation to the "subject-object split." Man's natural self-transcendence *creates* the subject-object relationship. It appears as the result of a certain degree of self-transcendence. No degree of this natural process can itself overcome or transcend the subject-object duality. However, ecstatic self-transcendence achieves exactly this: it overcomes the subject-object split without annihilating it.[34] This elevation beyond the subject-object scheme is necessary for the actualizing of unambiguous life.[35] The ecstasy of reason (or revelation) means to Tillich the transcendence of the ordinary struc-

---

34. Cf. Tillich, *Systematic Theology,* III, p. 92.
35. *Ibid.,* p. 76.

ture of reason, the subject-object structure.[36] Love between human beings cannot achieve union on the horizontal plane of
subjectivity and objectivity. It can only succeed in the vertical
dimension where each individual is elevated "above his self-relatedness." [37] In all of these areas, reconciliation or reunion requires an elevation beyond the subject-object split.

This achievement does not mean, in Tillich's account, the
direct reunion of subject and object. The attempt to realize the
dissolution of the subject in the objective world necessarily fails.
That with which self-relatedness is reunited "lies beyond subjectivity and objectivity." [38] Only when subject and object are
both reunited with the ground which transcends them can the
destructive tensions of subjectivity and objectivity be overcome.
Wherever this reunion occurs within existence, there the "holy"
appears; and once again the determinative characteristic of the
holy is its transcendence of the subject-object structure.[39]

Tillich's distinction then is between that natural self-transcendence whereby life goes out from itself in free self-creativity,
and that self-transcendence whereby both poles of life's self-
relatedness are elevated beyond themselves into a transcendent
unity with the ground of being. The former is the basis for the
movement of the creation outside of the divine life and for the
"fall" of man-and-his-world. It is also the basis for man's religion, his awareness of his infinity and his quest for it. But natural
self-transcendence remains ambigious and tragic; it cannot
achieve reconciliation. The power of ecstatic self-transcendence
must come from beyond the natural power of life, from the
ground of being, through the Divine Spirit.

We observed earlier that Tillich identifies divine and human
self-transcendence in one process of life. The question might be
asked here whether this identification is adequate to explain the
appearance of the Divine Spirit within the conditions of exist-

36. Cf. Tillich, *Systematic Theology*, I, p. 112.
37. Tillich, *Systematic Theology*, III, p. 261.
38. *Ibid.*, p. 253.
39. Cf. Tillich, *Systematic Theology*, I, pp. 214–216.

ence. The divine life empowers finitude with the ability to transcend itself, and this is consumated in human freedom. But is there not another divine going-out-from-itself which by becoming manifest in existence achieves reconciliation? Is not the initial process of life broken and tragic? Is not another divine self-transcendence necessary to explain reconciliation? Or can the single process of life be elevated beyond itself by a "new" infusion of divine power? The question of the relation between the divine life and finite life will bear closer examination in the succeeding chapters. The issue as to whether Tillich conceives the divine life to be complete in itself or whether it is completed only through the reconciliation of the creature will require further detailed comment.

In all dimensions, the power of being to overcome estrangement and ambiguity is the power of love. Indeed, for Tillich, the power of separation and of reunion is the power of love; for love is the power of life. "Life is being in actuality and love is the moving power of life." [40] Love is "the essence of life itself, namely, the dynamic reunion of that which is separated."[41] Love drives toward separation in order to fulfill itself as reunion of the separated. Ultimately, it is God's life which separates itself from itself and returns to itself, thus fulfilling the divine love through overcoming the most radical separation.

The Question of Pantheism

Tillich's system of thought, as described in outline here, would seem to be absolutely unique on the American scene—indeed, in contemporary theology generally. We have suggested the broad tradition within which Tillich stands. We might call attention here to the influence upon Tillich of the *Early Theological Writings* of Hegel, surveyed briefly in Chapter I. We com-

40. Tillich, *Love, Power, and Justice*, p. 25.
41. Tillich, *The Protestant Era*, p. xli; cf. Tillich, "Ist eine Wissenschaft von den Werten Möglich?" in *Zeitschrift für Evangelische Ethik* (May, 1961), p. 175, where love is described as the "universale Dynamik des Lebens."

mented upon the fact that Tillich relates his concept of life to that developed in these writings by Hegel. Tillich further suggests that Hegel "started in his early fragments as a philosopher of love," and that Hegel's dialectical pattern of thought "is an abstraction from his concrete intuition into the nature of love as separation and reunion." [42] This means that prior to the separation there is an original unity. Unity, including the unity between God and the world, is more basic for Hegel and Tillich than separation. Heterogeneity can never be unified; man's separation from God is, finally, a form of self-estrangement.

The suggestion that Tillich's theological position is, in many respects, close to that prefigured in Hegel's early writings brings to light what is probably the most fundamental theological criticism of Tillich's system: the assertion that it is pantheistic. In describing Hegel's earliest original philosophical position, Richard Kroner, in his introduction to the early writings, speaks of Hegel's "Pantheism of Love." [43] He states:

Hegel's Pantheism of Love has all the characteristics of his future metaphysic. It aims at the reconciliation of opposites, tries to overcome one-sided rationalism, one-sided emotionalism, or one-sided empiricism. It is dialectical in its structure, although its method is not yet dialectical in the strict sense of the word.[44]

Could much the same be said of Tillich's system? Is it pantheism?

Various critics have interpreted Tillich's thought as pantheistic. This supposed pantheism has been identified with both naturalism and idealism. Thus Sidney Hook, in a recent article, accuses Tillich of a "refurbishing of the myths of German idealism, including the romantic and magical idealism of the German *Natur-philosophen.*"[45] Tillich's unconditioned is the God of

42. Tillich, *Love, Power, and Justice,* p. 22.
43. Kroner writing in the introduction to Hegel, *"On Christianity . . . ,* p. 11.
44. *Ibid.,* p. 12.
45. Sidney Hook, "The Atheism of Paul Tillich," in *Religious Experience and Truth: A Symposium,* ed. by Sidney Hook, p. 59.

pantheistic spiritualism. "For all his talk of God as an 'unconditioned transcendent,' Tillich's God is the all-in-all of pantheistic spiritualism." [46] John Herman Randall, on the other hand, interprets Tillich's concept of God in a naturalistic way. He suggests that it is possible to interpret Tillich's ground of being as "the religious dimension of the world," [47] thus viewing Tillich's thought in terms of his own naturalism.

In order to evaluate this criticism we must first examine the ways in which God transcends the world (and the world, God), according to Tillich. At one point he suggests that there are two aspects to this transcendence: the divinity of God and the freedom of man.

God is immanent in the world as its permanent creative ground and is transcendent to the world through freedom. Both infinite divinity and finite human freedom make the world transcendent to God and God transcendent to the world.[48]

If our analysis is correct, the divinity of God, which makes him transcendent, is closely associated with the quality of holiness, in Tillich's view. Holiness "is the most adequate basis we have for understanding the divine. The holy and the divine must be interpreted correlatively." [49] The holiness of God is, in turn, significantly characterized by transcendence of the subject-object relationship. This, according to Tillich, is the meaning of Rudolph Otto's concept of the "numinous."

When Otto calls the experience of the holy "numinous," he interprets the holy as the presence of the divine. When he points to the mysterious character of holiness, he indicates that the holy transcends the subject-object structure of reality.[50]

God as holy is the ground of the self-world and subject-object polarities and thus cannot be brought within them. As mysticism

46. *Ibid.,* p. 60.
47. J. H. Randall, Jr., *The Role of Knowledge in Western Religion,* p. 124; cf. pp. 130–134.
48. Tillich, *Systematic Theology,* I, p. 263.
49. *Ibid.,* p. 215.
50. *Ibid.,* pp. 215–216.

has frequently affirmed, God remains subject, even when he appears to become object, indicating that the relation to God transcends the subject-object relation.

The holiness of God as thus interpreted has religious as well as cognitive implications. In Tillich's view, the courage to be "must be rooted in a power of being that is greater than the power of oneself and the power of one's world." [51] Power derived from one pole of the self-world polarity tends to destroy the other pole; one loses either oneself as subject or one's participation in one's world. This analysis is the basis for Tillich's critique of theism. God as the absolute subject tends to destroy man's subjectivity by making him into an object exclusively for God as subject. The true God is neither subject nor object, and his power is the ground of both self and world. It is this transcendence of the self-world polarity which Tillich seeks to symbolize in the concept of the divine life. It is this form of transcendence which, according to Tillich's position, prevents an identification of God and nature, at least nature as viewed objectively. Likewise, God cannot be viewed as the Supreme Subject. God cannot be brought into the subject-object relationship; he cannot be "thingified," or made into a subject.

Various classical versions of pantheism, however, have avoided the inclusion of God within the subject-object relationship. Thus God, or Nature, according to Spinoza, has the attributes of both thought and extension. The assertion that God transcends subjectivity and objectivity does not necessarily eliminate pantheism. God can transcend the world of subjects and objects and still not be ontologically separate from it.

The second way in which God transcends the world for Tillich has to do with the reality of human freedom. God transcends the world (or the world transcends God) because of the reality of finite freedom, which makes the world in some sense independent of God. Tillich seems to distinguish his thought

51. Tillich, *The Courage to Be*, p. 155.

from the pantheism of Spinoza by maintaining that Spinoza's system eliminates freedom.

> Spinoza establishes a naturalistic pantheism . . . which denies finite freedom and in so doing denies the freedom of God. By necessity God is merged into finite beings, and their being in his being. Here again it must be emphasized that pantheism does not say that God is everything. It says that God is the substance of everything and that there is no substantial independence and freedom in anything finite.[52]

Elsewhere he states that it is the presence of finite freedom within the world which makes pantheism impossible.[53]

It would appear, then, that Tillich seeks explicitly to defend his thought against the charge of pantheism primarily through his concept of finite freedom. We have noted that freedom for Tillich is closely associated with self-transcendence. In this context his position seems to be that the ontological separation involved in the realization of finite freedom makes pantheism impossible. However, as we shall see, human self-transcendence and freedom can be viewed in Tillich's thought as a manifestation of the divine self-transcendence and freedom. If this is the case, is there a genuine ontological separation? The issue of pantheism does hinge upon the nature of the ontological separation of the world from God (based upon freedom). We shall seek to show that Tillich's answer to this question is to be found in the relation of the divine life to human life. We shall seek to shed light on this problem through a more careful analysis of the nature of the ontological separation which occurs through self-transcendence and freedom.

This concludes our broad survey of Tillich's system and of certain critical problems connected with it. We now turn to a more detailed consideration of Tillich's concept of estrangement.

---

52. Tillich, *Systematic Theology*, I, pp. 237–238.
53. Tillich, *Systematic Theology*, II, p. 8.

the experiment
in elevation

IT WAS pointed out in Chapter One that Tillich views the analysis of estranged existence as the task of existentialism. Any study of Tillich's understanding of estrangement, then, might well begin with an interpretation of Tillich's approach to the existentialist analysis. It was further suggested in Chapter One that Tillich's theological method might best be interpreted as an "elevation" of non-theological ideas of estrangement through the application of the criterion of self-estrangement. In his systematic treatise employing the method of correlation, Tillich does not deal explicitly with specific existentialist analyses; nor does he anywhere explicitly employ the criterion of self-estrangement as outlined here. The purpose of this chapter will be to show that this criterion is actually involved in the application of the method of correlation. This attempt will consist of two parts: an illustration of the fact that Tlilich does implicitly use this criterion in certain specific comments concerning existentialist views of estrangement; and a demonstration of the fact that it can be effectively used in implementing the method, by engaging in a detailed critique of Fromm's view of alienation from a Tillichian point of view.

Does Tillich Employ This Criterion?

In a broad consideration of existentialism from Tillich's point of view, our starting point is his contention, cited in Chapter

One, that the existentialists agree in understanding the human problem as estrangement. This we shall accept as a legitimate generalization. However, Tillich's implicit assumption, also cited above, that all existentialists conceive of alienation as total, or, in Tillich's terms, as self-estrangement, must be rejected. As we have seen, Tillich concedes that this is not the case; but he defines all departures from the perspective of total estrangement as departures from existentialism. We are maintaining, then, that Tillich defines existentialism according to his own criterion and rejects all other aspects of the writings of this group as non-existentialist. We shall now demonstrate how Tillich applies this criterion by analyzing certain of his remarks concerning specific existentialists.

Rather than finding agreement among the existentialists in understanding alienation as self-alienation, it would appear that Tillich finds at least two schools of thought within existentialism which depart in opposite directions from this understanding. We shall, for the sake of our discussion, call these schools the "radical" existentialists and the "utopian" existentialists. (Tillich uses these terms in an incidental way.) The radical group, as interpreted by Tillich, tends to emphasize the totality of alienation to the point where no reconciliation is possible. Here alienation becomes identified with finite human nature as such. Tillich places Nietzsche, Heidegger, Jaspers, Bergson, and Sartre in this category.[1] In this view, human nature as such is incurable; man cannot be "healed" or "saved." Tillich, in a discussion of Sartre and Heidegger, identifies this view as the failure to distinguish between "essence" and "existence."

Sartre says man's essence is his existence. In saying this he makes it impossible for man to be saved or to be healed. . . . Heidegger talks also as if there were no norms whatsoever, no essential man, as if man makes himself.[2]

1. Tillich, "Existential Philosophy: Its Historical Meaning," in *Theology of Culture,* p. 102; cf. "The Theological Significance of Existentialism and Psychoanalysis," in *Theology of Culture,* p. 121, for Sartre.
2. Tillich, "The Theological Significance . . . ," *Theology of Culture,* p. 121.

Tillich interprets Sigmund Freud's concept of "libido" as another view of human nature as essentially tragic.[3]

Tillich challenges these views by maintaining that any concept of man as estranged must presuppose some idea of man as healed or reconciled. He argues that the radical existentialists do assume an idea of essential man, the view that man is not what he ought to be. Tillich holds that this idea is inconsistent with the tragic view of human nature. Concerning Sartre and Heidegger, he writes:

But here also [in Sartre] we have a happy inconsistency. He calls his existentialism humanism. But if he calls it humanism, that means he has an idea of what man essentially is, and he must consider the possibility that the essential being of man, his freedom, might be lost. . . . [Heidegger] speaks of the difference between authentic existence and unauthentic existence, falling into the average existence of conventional thought and nonsense—into an existence where he has lost himself.[4]

Freud also was inconsistent in this respect.

Now, fortunately, Freud, like most great men, was not consistent. With respect to the healing process, he knew something about the healed man. . . . In popular terms, his pessimism about the nature of man and his optimism about the possibilities of healing were not reconciled in him or his followers.[5]

While these statements are too fragmentary to serve effectively as critiques of the existentialist philosophies mentioned, they do reveal something of Tillich's attitude toward them. First, he holds that if one conceives of existing man as alienated, he must "in some way presuppose an idea of his essential nature." Secondly, he holds that all of the radical existentialists believe, at times inconsistently, that man can be healed, that the split

3. *Ibid.*, pp. 119–120; for other tragic views of existence cf. Tillich's comments about Buddhism and "radical mysticism" in *Systematic Theology*, II, pp. 70–72.
4. Tillich, "The Theological Significance . . . ," *Theology of Culture*, p. 121.
5. *Ibid.*, p. 120.

between essence and present existence can be overcome. When Tillich calls them inconsistent, he seems to mean that their concepts of alienation are such that the healing of human nature is impossible. For example, Tillich interprets Freud's concept of libido as a desire which can never be satisfied and which therefore produces a desire for death. Thus Tillich interprets the radical existentialists as attempting to affirm at the same time the totality of alienation and the possibility of healing. The concept of self-estrangement can be proposed as a means of preserving these two emphases.

We must now consider the other group, which we have called the "utopian" existentialists. This group rejects the view of Hegel that reconciliation has already been achieved; but it is united in holding the view that estrangment is a characteristic of present-day society which can be overcome through subsequent social or psychological development. This conviction, which Tillich terms utopian, can, he thinks, be found at an early stage in the existentialist protest against Hegel in the writings of Marx. Tillich writes:

But estrangement is not for him [Marx] an inevitable tragic necessity. It is the product of a special historical situation, and can be overcome through human action. It is in this attitude that the Utopian elements of the later Marxist movements are rooted.[6]

This optimism about human possibilities is paralleled in the writings of some of the followers of Freud, as Tillich interprets them. These men (Tillich mentions Carl Jung and Fromm in this context) have, according to Tillich, abandoned Freud's insight concerning the depth of human estrangement, that is, the ideas "about existential libido and the death instinct." In so doing, according to Tillich, they have lost the depth and profundity in Freud's analysis of the human predicament. What Tillich apparently means here is not that these men have abandoned the Freudian insights concerning libido and the death instinct alto-

6. Tillich, "Existential Philosophy . . . ," *Theology of Culture*, p. 103.

gether (as we have seen, Fromm, for example, does not reject the death instinct completely), but that they have rejected the idea of existential libido and the death instinct as universally present in all men. They view the human situation of estrangement as "correctable and amendable, as a weakness only," susceptible to change on the individual level through psychiatric techniques and on the social level through social reform.

Those psychoanalysts, such as Fromm, who relate man's alienation (and the consequent regressive impulses) to the structure of present-day society can be grouped with the Marxists in failing to see the universal character of man's estrangement. Concerning such analyses Tillich writes:

There are many sociological and existentialist analyses of man in industrial society which point to self-loss and world-loss, to mechanization and objectification, to emptiness and meaninglessness. These analyses are true as far as they go, but they are fallacious if in our period of history they derive the evil of man's predicament from the structure of industrial society. Such a derivation implies the belief that changes in the structure of our society would, as such, change man's existential predicament. All utopianism has this character; its main mistake is in not distinguishing man's existential situation from its manifestation in different historical periods.[7]

Tillich explicitly places Fromm in the category of the utopians. In a review of Fromm's *The Sane Society*, Tillich evaluates the fact that Fromm's work is centered around the concept of aliention:

I want to ask a question about the meaning of Fromm's term "alienation," especially because my own theological thought centers partly around the synonomous concept "estrangement." It seems to me that there is a difference between Christian theology and humanist psychology in this respect in spite of the use of synonomous terms. Alienation, for Fromm, is a necessity of man's development and therefore something that can be overcome in the process of this development. In the "Sane Society" alienation is conquered. Theology would call the anticipation of such a society within history utopian. . . . For theology, estrangement is the characteristic of man's pre-

7. Tillich, *Systematic Theology*, II, p. 74.

dicament in time and space . . . life by its very nature unites creative and destructive elements.[8]

The utopians, then, according to Tillich, do not see that estrangement is total. In holding it to be correctable by human effort, they implicitly exempt some aspect of human life from the effects of alienation. The concept of self-estrangement retains the idea that estrangement is correctable but denies that this can be achieved by human effort.

Thus it is apparent that the existentialists do not agree on the application of the idea of estrangement. It is certainly not the case that all existentialists understand estrangement as self-estrangement in the sense employed by Tillich. On the contrary, Tillich is forced to defend his concept of self-estrangement in two directions: against the radical existentialists, he holds that alienation is not a characteristic of human nature as such; against the utopian existentialists, he holds that it is a "characteristic of man's predicament in time and space." In order to maintain the position that alienation is completely serious, but that human nature as such is not tragic, Tillich employs, implicitly and explicitly, the concept of self-estrangement. No estrangement which is less than self-estrangement can be completely serious; but self-estrangement is still estrangement and is therefore not essentially tragic. We shall see that this view of estrangement leads Tillich to the distinction between "essential finitude" and "existential estrangement," and to the possibility of their fragmentary reunion in "unambiguous life." It also leads him ultimately to the concept of the divine self-estrangement and self-reconciliation.

A Critique of Fromm's Concept of Alienation

We concluded in Chapter Six that alienation in Fromm's view is partial rather than total and cannot, therefore, be called self-estrangement. In the preceding section we indicated that Tillich

8. Tillich, "Erich Fromm's *The Sane Society,*" *Pastoral Psychology,* VI (September, 1955), p. 14.

designates such ideas of estrangement and reconciliation as utopian; and we suggested in Chapter One that if Tillich's apologetic method is to operate effectively with regard to such works, he must seek to show that the symptoms of estrangement identified by the utopian existentialists themselves actually necessitate a more serious alienation than these analysts are willing to grant. We shall now seek to show how, from Tillich's point of view, this criticism might be applied in detail to the work of Fromm.

An analysis of Fromm's work from this perspective is worthwhile, not only because of the structural similarities in the thought of the two men, but also because of the specific content which Fromm gives to the idea of estrangement. Fromm focuses attention on a symptom of alienation which is clearly a fundamental characteristic of it: the experience of loneliness which accompanies conscious individuality. Alienation for Fromm, as indeed for all who employ the term, is separation, and therefore Fromm concludes that alienation as experienced is first of all loneliness and isolation. We might legitimately speak of loneliness in Fromm's thought as the affective side of alienation.

Because separation is painful, Fromm also sees a flight from loneliness into some infantile or immature organic or social unity. This attempt is never finally successful, but it does serve to alleviate loneliness. In any case, the various forms of "symbiotic" union described by Fromm are attempts to solve the problem posed by alienation. They are "answers" to the human problem, not a part of the problem itself. Fromm's categories remain evolutionary; the basic structure is the movement from a primal unity through separation and loneliness to a new unity on a higher level. Return to the primal unities is regression rather than alienation. Human nature drives toward unity with the "all," with nature; but unity on the highest level requires a temporary separation, and consequent loneliness. One goes out in order to return enriched. Separation, though painful, is a progressive step.

Tillich also gives a prominent place to the experience of lone-liness as one of the major results of estrangement.[9] However, he consistently sees loneliness in interdependence with "submerg-ence" in various types of collective. The former leads to a loss of the sense of sharing, the latter to the loss of individuality or subjectivity. Tillich holds that these experiences drive toward each other.

In the state of estrangement man is shut within himself and cut off from participation. At the same time, he falls under the power of objects which tend to make him into a mere object without a self. If subjectivity separates itself from objectivity, the objects swallow the empty shell of subjectivity.

This situation has been described sociologically and psycholog-ically. These descriptions have shown the interdependence of the loneliness of the individual and his submergence in the collective in a convincing way.[10]

Tillich holds that this alternation between loneliness and sub-mergence or hostility and surrender is a sign of estrangement from man's true or essential nature. It is man's nature to exist in a polar relationship of what he calls "solitude" on the one hand and "participation" or "communion" on the other. Solitude be-longs to a being which is structurally centered; as far as man is concerned, this means self-consciousness.

It is necessary to distinguish essential and existential structures of aloneness. Every living being is structurally centered; man has a com-pletely centered self. This centeredness cuts him off from the whole of reality which is not identified with himself. He is alone in the world and the more so, the more he is conscious of himself as him-self.[11]

But in essential man this centeredness is the basis for partici-pation.

On the other hand, his complete centeredness enables him to par-ticipate in his world without limits; and love, as the dynamic power

9. Tillich, *Systematic Theology*, I, pp. 199–200; *Systematic Theology*, II, pp. 65–66, 71–72.
10. Tillich, *Systematic Theology*, II, p. 65.
11. *Ibid.*, p. 71.

of life, drives him toward such participation. . . . Only he who is able to have solitude is able to have communion.[12]

The perfection of one pole, the individual person, involves the perfection of the other pole, the communal society.

Tillich understands loneliness to be the result of a breach of the polar relation between solitude and communion. When solitude becomes loneliness, communion becomes submergence.

Finite individualization produces a dynamic tension with finite participation; the break of their unity is a possibility. Self-relatedness produces the threat of a loneliness in which world and communion are lost. On the other hand, being in the world and participating in it produces the threat of a complete collectivization, a loss of individuality and subjectivity whereby the self loses its self-relatedness and is transformed into a mere part of an embracing whole.[13]

The estranged man alternates between lonely isolation on the one hand and submergence and loss of self in the collective on the other.

Thus, for Tillich, both lonely isolation and submergence in the collective are marks of estrangement. Since it would appear that Tillich's concept of submergence is quite comparable to Fromm's concept of regression, we can say that for Tillich both regression and isolation are marks of alienation. We have noted in Chapter Six that Fromm is at times inclined to speak of regression as alienation, but we have also noted the difficulties which this poses for his evolutionary scheme. In his terms, if alienation is to be a form of separation from nature, it cannot at the same time be a form of reunion with nature. Yet Fromm sees that both of these conditions, loneliness and symbiotic union, represent a failure to realize man's full nature; and he sees that man is driven in dissatisfaction and distress from one pole to the other.

It might be argued, then, that the empirical data recognized by Fromm require a concept of alienation which includes both isolation and submergence or regression. In Fromm's formulation, the

12. *Ibid.*
13. Tillich, *Systematic Theology,* I, p. 199.

man who is alienated has lost only "communion" or union. But according to the data as interpreted here he has lost true solitude as well. And, in like fashion, the man who regresses has lost not only "solitude" or individuality, but also communion or participation. The two states are interdependent. If this is the case, the separation referred to in the concept of alienation cannot be equated with the separation of man from the primal unities with nature. Otherwise, regression to these unities (whether through father or mother figure, clan, etc.,) would not be alienation. Some other separation must be responsible for alienation, a separation which transmutes man's solitude into isolation and his communion into submergence. The task set for Tillich's analysis by this approach is the formulation of a concept of alienation which could result in both isolation and submergence.

In order to do this, Tillich moves beyond the concept of alienation as self-consciousness to show that man's "participation," including unconscious participation, as well as his "separation," that is, his consciousness, is alienated. If separation has become loneliness, participation has become submergence or the loss of individuality. To indicate this development in his thought we must summarize his concept of the "self," for it is not consciousness, but the self in its totality, which has become alienated, in Tillich's view. Tillich uses the term "self" in a broader sense than the psychoanalytic term "ego"; he does not identify self and consciousness.

The term "self" is more embracing than the term "ego." It includes the subconscious and the unconscious "basis" of the self-conscious ego as well as self-consciousness (*cogitatio* in the Cartesian sense). . . . Man is a fully developed and completely centered self. He "possesses" himself in the form of self-consciousness. He has an ego-self.[14]

The concept of self includes both individuality and participation.

Being a self means being separated in some way from everything else, having everything else opposite one's self, being able to look

14. *Ibid.*, pp. 169–170.

at it and to act upon it. At the same time, however, this self is aware that it belongs to that at which it looks. The self is "in" it.[15]

Being a centered being means having an environment; being an ego-self means having a "world." And this "world" is not an entity unrelated to the ego-self, but is correlative with it.

Because man has an ego-self, he transcends every possible environment. Man has a world. Like environment, world is a correlative concept. Man *has* a world, although he is in it at the same time. "World" is not the sum total of all beings—an inconceivable concept. As the Greek *kosmos* and the Latin *universum* indicate, "world" is a structure or a unity of manifoldness. If we say that man has a world at which he looks, from which he is separated and to which he belongs, we think of a structured whole even though we may describe this world in pluralistic terms.[16]

As we have seen, Tillich holds that this interdependence of ego-self and world is an irreducible structure of reality, the key to ontology. This polarity, and with it the subject-object relationship, cannot be derived from one side or the other; it is a fundamental, not a derivative, distinction.

For our purposes, it is important to note Tillich's view that the self can be comprehended only by seeing it in a "complex dialectical relationship." This complex structure of the self is the basis for the polarity of individualization and participation, as well as subject and object. It is also the basis for the fact that neither is more primary, nor can one be derived from the other. It is the essential nature of the self to hold these two poles in a harmonious relationship. But the self is also the being which can lose itself if the polarity of individuality and participation is lost. This means, in the context of our discussion, that for Tillich man is *essentially* an individual as well as a participant. This dialectical conception of the self enables Tillich to hold that man in estrangement is still both individual and participant but that both aspects of his nature have become estranged. Individuality has become isolation and participation has become submergence.

15. *Ibid.*, p. 170.
16. *Ibid.*

Reconciliation means the re-establishment of the polarity of solitude and community. Fromm's position, on the other hand, associates alienation closely with individuality. This prevents his understanding submergence as a form of alienation and also makes it difficult for him to indicate how individuality may be preserved when alienation is overcome.

If a self becomes alienated, Tillich maintains that at the same time the self's world, which it "has" and is "in," has also become alienated. The destructive separation of ego-self and world is not estrangement but the result of the estrangement of the self-and-its-world. Since the self reaches into the world through participation, the world cannot remain unaffected if the total self is alienated. Tillich holds that the participation of man in all levels of nature and in human society must be taken seriously. He cites four reasons for this:

First, it can be shown that in the development of man there is no absolute discontinuity between animal bondage and human freedom. . . . Second, one cannot decide at which points in the development of the human individual responsibility begins and ends. . . . Third, we must refer to the present rediscovery of the unconscious and its determining power in man's decisions. . . . Fourth, the social dimension of unconscious strivings must be considered. The questionable term "collective unconscious" points to the reality of this dimension.[17]

This participation does not negate individuality but it does limit it. Tillich holds that by virtue of mutual participation, and in spite of individualization, all being is a unity. After asking a series of questions implying man's participation in nature and other men, Tillich writes:

These questions show that the element of participation in the polarity of individualization and participation must be considered much more seriously with respect to the mutual participation of nature and man. . . . What happens in the microcosm happens by mutual participation in the macrocosmos, for being itself is one.[18]

17. Tillich, *Systematic Theology*, II, pp. 41–42.
18. Tillich, *Systematic Theology*, I, p. 261.

If man is estranged from his true nature or essence, then nature also, the world which man has, must be estranged.

We must ask here whether Tillich means that nature is constituted as existent (and therefore fallen) by man's consciousness of it. Is it man's consciousness which carries nature "outside" the divine life? If this were the case, it would be fair to say of Tillich as we said of Fromm that alienation is caused by self- and world-consciousness. Is self-consciousness the effective instrument of self-transcendence, and thus of alienation, for Tillich?

Here as elsewhere Tillich's answer involves a structural polarity—in this case the polarity of freedom and destiny. Man in freedom affirms the movement of self-actualization which carries him and his world outside the divine life. Indeed, man's consciousness of his finitude (hence, anxiety) is "one of the driving forces toward the transition from essence to existence." [19] In spite of his emphasis on man's free choice for actualization, however, it would appear that for Tillich the pole of destiny, the dynamic movement of being toward self-transcendence, is the primary "driving force" in the transition. Consciousness is viewed primarily as a "mirror" of the ontological process rather than the substance of the process itself. The "fallenness" of existence is rooted in the drive of being toward individualization and is thus not constituted by consciousness, although it is affirmed and chosen by human freedom. In Tillich's view, the transition from essence to existence is a movement in being, not just a development within consciousness.

Let us summarize the results of our discussion. We saw that Fromm can be said to identify loneliness as the affective side of alienation. He also describes the regressive attempts to escape loneliness, and at times he speaks of these as alienation also. But in his thought a distinction must be made between them. Since man emerges out of a primal unity, the achievement of separation accompanied by loneliness is a progressive step, though it results in alienation; whereas the flight from loneliness is regres-

19. Tillich, *Systematic Theology*, II, p. 35.

sive. In Fromm's later usage he reserves the term "alienation" for the progressive step.

Tillich, on the other hand, sees loneliness and submergence in the collective as interdependent. He feels that this view is supported by the sociological and psychological data, though at the same time it can also be derived from his concept of man's essential nature. Tillich holds that man is essentially both individual and participant, in polar relation. The being which is most separate is the being which can participate most fully. Since in man's essential nature these poles are harmoniously balanced, if one is lost both are lost.

If the self becomes alienated, this means, according to Tillich, that this polar structure of "individualization" and "participation" arises out of, and becomes estranged from, some primal unity. This prior unity cannot be either "world" or "ego-self," for these are interdependent. We must conceive a source which is "beyond existence," beyond self and world.

Furthermore, if these poles of individualization and participation are interdependent, one cannot be derived from the other. They are both fundamental aspects of the structure of the self. Estrangement cannot consist simply of lonely isolation. It is rather a separation from the "original" harmonious relation of individualization and participation which constitutes the essential nature of the self. This separation can result in either lonely isolation or self-escaping submergence. Reconciliation is then the re-establishment of this harmonious polar relation.

The self, again, has a world to which it at the same time belongs (a world which includes the social and historical context). Therefore, whatever happens to the self happens to the world also. If the self is estranged we must speak of the world as estranged also. The world which man has is not that from which he is estranged; it participates in the estrangement.

We proposed in this analysis to show how the symptoms of estrangement described by Fromm actually point to an alienation more serious than Fromm admits. We have sought to do this in Tillich's terms by showing that it is not just self-consciousness, but the self-in-its-world, which becomes estranged. If estrangement is total, if man and his world are estranged, we must consider the possibility of a reconciliation which comes to man from beyond his existence altogether. Existence is a question, not an answer. Man is self-estranged.

This critique of Fromm from a Tillichian viewpoint raises, in turn, important questions concerning Tillich's analysis. These questions center around the meaning of self-estrangement. Tillich's apologetic theology must show that, although existence itself is estranged, it is not separated from some alien being, but from its own essential nature. This separation Tillich seeks to describe through the "symbols" of the Christian message. We now turn to a survey of Tillich's effort to correlate the Christian answers with the existential questions.

tillich's theological answers: part one

Essential Man, Existential Man, and the "New Being"

TILLICH proposes, in his theological method, to correlate the questions raised by the existentialist analysis with the theological answers derived from the Christian message. As we have seen, the proper sphere of existentialism has been defined by Tillich as the analysis and description of alienation. Any answers given to the problem posed by alienation must be derived from some positive religious tradition. This separation of existentialist question and theological answer presented us with an apparent dilemma: to what extent, if any, does existentialist analysis as such know man's essential nature, or his true fulfillment? On the one hand, Tillich suggests that no knowledge of man's estrangement is possible without some concept of his essential nature and of the possibility of healing or salvation. On the other hand, Tillich views knowledge of man's essential nature as a part of the theological "answer."

In the interpretation of the method which we have proposed, autonomous ideas of estrangement and reconciliation actually presuppose the theological doctrines and are based upon some revelation, however fragmentary, of God or "being-itself," of essential human nature, and of the "New Being." By this line of thought, a fragmentary knowledge of what man ought to be, and of the possibility of "healing," is attainable by existentialist an-

alysis; but its knowledge of the nature of man's estrangement
will also be fragmentary.

Existentialism, according to this view, is at least dimly aware
of three concepts which Tillich holds to be fundamental to the
Christian tradition: the concepts of creation, the "fall," and the
possibility of salvation.

In the Christian tradition, there are three fundamental concepts.
First: *Esse qua esse bonum est*. This Latin phrase is a basic dogma of
Christianity. It means "Being as being is good," or in the Biblical
mythological form: God saw everything that he had created, and
behold, it was good. The second statement is the universal fall—fall
meaning the transition from this essential goodness into existential
estrangement from oneself, which happens in every living being and
in every time. The third statement refers to the possibility of salva-
ion. We should remember that salvation is derived from *salvus* or
salus in Latin, which means "healed" or "whole," as opposed to dis-
ruptiveness.[1]

These theological concepts can be rendered philosophically.

Now in philosophical terms, this means that man's essential and existential nature points to his teleological nature.[2]

As Tillich states, it is not the complete failure to discern these
elements, but the confusion of them, for which existentialism
must be criticized (or elevated beyond itself).

Every criticism of existentialism and psychoanalysis on the basis of
this tripartite view of human nature is directed against the confusion
of these three fundamental elements, which always must be distinguished although they always are together in all of us.[3]

The task of theological analysis here, then, is primarily to distinguish essence from existence, since man's teleological nature
represents their reunion.

At this point we reach another basic problem in the interpretation of Tillich's categories. We have observed that for Tillich

1. Tillich, "The Theological Significance...," *Theology of Culture*,
pp. 118–119.
   2. *Ibid.*, p. 119.
   3. *Ibid.*

the analysis of existence is analysis of estrangement, for existence is estrangement. But we have also noted Tillich's view that the existentialist must assume the reality of man's essential nature in order to view him as estranged. The error which theology must seek to prevent is the confusion of essence and existence.

This position must now be combined with Tillich's acknowledgment that essence and existence are ambiguously mixed in actual "life." Somewhat unexpectedly from the viewpoint of common usage Tillich's term "existence" is revealed to be an abstraction from concrete actuality. What effect does this have upon our argument that estrangement for Tillich must be total—a self-estrangement? Is not life accurately portrayed as a confused mixture of essential and existential elements, and thus as only partially estranged?

Tillich's answer involves his understanding of the dialectical structure of life. As we have seen, life is conceived as the movement from potentiality toward actuality. This is not an unambiguous process, however, for in this movement life becomes estranged from itself. Tillich's position can be expressed this way: finite reality, insofar as it is not mere potential and insofar as it has not achieved a fragmentary reunion, is estranged. Furthermore, this existence is a stage through which all life passes; no dimension of life is exempt. Thus estrangement is total in the sense that all aspects of life are affected. All aspects of life need "salvation." At the same time, life in concrete actuality combines potential, existential, and unambiguously fulfilled elements.

Tillich's account with existentialism can now be settled before we proceed. It would seem that our earlier point has been verified: Tillich cannot satisfactorily confine existentialism to an analysis of existence, which he concedes is an abstraction. Existentialism analyzes life, which combines the three elements cited above, although it may focus upon the problems of existence. Its knowledge of all three is based upon religious insight, which may, however, be attenuated and inadequate. It would appear that a systematic distinction between existentialism and philosophies of life cannot be maintained. Both seek the New Being within existence, and both seek unambiguous life. Indeed, Tillich interprets both (and modern ontology as well) to be rooted in the Hegelian insight concerning the dialectical property of life. Tillich's dialogue or correlation is thus mainly with one general trend of modern thought, although admittedly an important one.

Our task now is to show how, in Tillich's view, the symbols of the Christian message—creation, the fall, and salvation—best account for the possibility and the actuality of self-estrangement. In other words, we must show how the Christian symbols deal with the relationship of essence and existence. We begin with a few preliminary remarks concerning "revelation."

As we have seen, Tillich holds that knowledge of man's essential nature is a religious "answer." As such, it is known, not through reason, but through "revelation." Revelation for Tillich is not esoteric knowledge of divine objects. Rather, it is a kind of knowledge where the usual subject-object relation is transcended, and union is achieved. The event of revelation is "ecstatic" in the sense that the mind literally transcends its ordinary structure. Ecstasy in the mind is correlated with "miracle" in reality, an event which points to that in being which transcends the self-world polarity, the "ground of being." Revelation is a manifestation, not of something of casual interest, but of that which "concerns us ultimately." [4] According to Tillich, revelation is at the same time "salvation," in the sense of healing, the reunion of man with that from which he has been separated.

Thus, for our purposes, revelation in Tillich's view may be understood as the overcoming of estrangement, the reuniting of man with his own essential nature, which, as we shall see, is inseparable from reunion with the ground of being. If revelation is salvation, no detached secular philosophy will have access to it; by the same token, any philosophy which offers a legitimate

4. For Tillich's discussion of revelation cf. Tillich, *Systematic Theology,* I, pp. 106–126.

path toward the overcoming of estrangement must be based on those fragmentary revelatory and saving experiences which occur throughout history. It must be religious, even when in secular garb.[5]

Tillich's contention that reconciling knowledge must transcend the subject-object relation might be compared with Fromm's distinction between "intellection" and the knowledge which unites. The difference lies on the level of the self-world polarity. Tillich holds that the self, or subject, cannot find itself in the world, or object. It must be reconciled with that which transcends and is the ground for both self and world in order to be reconciled with the world. Since Fromm sees subject derived from object, from nature, it can find itself again in the object.

Tillich holds that no reconciling action can emerge from estranged existence.

In every act of existential self-realization, freedom and destiny are united. Existence is always both fact and act. From this it follows that no act within the context of existential estrangement can overcome existential estrangement. Destiny keeps freedom in bondage without eliminating it.[6]

An act stemming from an estranged reality cannot be a reconciling act. A new reality is required, and the question of revelation and salvation is the quest for such a reality.

It is the question of a reality in which the self-estrangement of our existence is overcome, a reality of reconciliation and reunion, of creativity, meaning, and hope. We shall call such a reality the "New Being." [7]

The Christian message, in the context of the human predicament understood as total estrangement, is the proclamation of the manifestation of the New Being in Jesus the Christ. As the Christ, Jesus represents the appearance of essential manhood under the conditions of existence. Tillich suggests that the very

5. Cf. Tillich, *Systematic Theology*, II, pp. 166–167.
6. *Ibid.*, p. 78.
7. Tillich, *Systematic Theology*, I, p. 49.

distinction between essential and existential man for Christian thought is made on the basis of their union discerned in the life of Jesus as the Christ. This implies again that in Tillich's view the distinction between essential and existential man is a religious insight based on revelation, however fragmentary.

The theological task, according to this interpretation of Tillich's thought, is the analytical separation of these elements, which are unified in Christ and present in partial distortion in all men. Since there was no time when essential man existed, Tillich turns to the Biblical myth of creation for a description of essential man "prior to" existence. It is necessary to use this myth, according to Tillich, because the being of essential or potential man must be spoken of as "prior to" actual existence.

The difficulty is that the state of essential being is not an actual stage of human development which can be known directly or indirectly. The essential nature of man is present in all stages of his development, although in existential distortion. In myth and dogma man's essential nature has been projected into the past as a history before history, symbolized as a golden age or paradise. In psychological terms one can interpret this state as that of "dreaming innocence." Both words point to something that precedes actual existence. It has potentiality, not actuality.[8]

Speaking mythologically, the significant aspect of Adam's condition was his unity with God. Speaking in terms of Tillich's "halfway demythologization," man, along with other beings, can be spoken of in his essential nature as a determinate "power of being" within the divine life. Man's essential nature has its being, symbolically speaking, within "the creative process of the divine life." [9] Essential man, then, has his being within the life of God, who is being-itself.

This unity of essential manhood with God has been recovered, according to Tillich's Christology, in the life of Christ. Indeed, unity with God is the outstanding characteristic of his life. This unity in one existing man is the Christian paradox. The achieve-

8. Tillich, *Systematic Theology*, II, p. 33.
9. Tillich, *Systematic Theology*, I, p. 255.

ment of this unity in Christ implies that there was "from the beginning" an essential or potential unity within the divine life.

The assertion that Jesus as the Christ is the personal unity of a divine and a human nature must be replaced by the assertion that in Jesus as the Christ the eternal unity of God and man has become historical reality. In his being, the New Being is real, and the New Being is the re-established unity between God and man.

. . . .

This event could not have taken place if there had not been an eternal unity of God and man within the divine life.[10]

Thus our analyses of the mythical Adam and the historical Christ bring us to the same point: essential man is man in unity with God. However, in Christ there is the further element of existence, and hence actuality; Christ is not simply a repetition of Adam. Tillich has asserted more clearly in Volume Three that there is something positive in existence which is gathered up into the "New Being."[11] The re-establishment of unity in existence is actual, after contest and decision.

Our analysis of man's essential nature viewed through the Christian tradition brings us to the conclusion, then, that for Tillich the separation of man from his essential nature is really the separation of man from God, understood as the ground of being or the power of being. This conclusion poses a problem for our analysis. We have spoken of Tillich's conception of estrangement as a self-estrangement, and have used this criterion in a critique of other views of estrangement. But if in Tillich's account man's estrangement from his essential nature is really an estrangement from God, in what sense can this be legitimately termed a self-estrangement? To answer this question we must analyze Tillich's understanding of finitude and its relation to God or being-itself. This analysis is, in fact, a further explication of Tillich's doctrine of creation, now expressed in ontological categories.

10. Tillich, *Systematic Theology*, II, p. 148.
11. Cf. Tillich, *Systematic Theology*, III, pp. 400–401.

Finitude, Infinity, and Being-Itself

According to Tillich, all beings, including man, are finite; this means that they are limited and threatened by nonbeing. This combination of being with the threat of nonbeing is the problem of finitude.

The dialectical problem of nonbeing is inescapable. It is the problem of finitude. Finitude unites being with dialectical nonbeing. Man's finitude, or creatureliness, is unintelligible without the concept of dialectical nonbeing.[12]

Finitude as such is not a mark of estrangement. It belongs to the essential nature of being. Thus man is essentially subject to threat but is not necessarily overcome by threat.

Finitude is the possibility of losing one's ontological structure and, with it, one's self. But this is a possibility, not a necessity. To be finite is to be threatened. But a threat is possibility, not actuality.[13]

Man is unique in experiencing his finitude by transcending it. By being aware of his finitude he is in some sense beyond it. But if finitude is transcended, this must point to a possible "infinity" or "nonfiniteness" in man. Tillich does not think of infinity in terms of an infinite being; in his view there is no infinite being, inasmuch as God is not *a* being at all. Infinity for Tillich is the unlimited self-transcendence of finitude.

As the negative character of the word indicates, [infinity] is defined by the dynamic and free self-transcendence of finite being.

.   .   .   .

Infinitude is finitude transcending itself without any a priori limit.[14]

Man in his awareness of his finitude, then, is aware of an infinity which is not foreign to his nature, since he already participates in it. At the same time his infinity makes him aware of his actual finitude. He concludes that though he is excluded from infinity, it is nevertheless something to which he naturally

12. Tillich, *Systematic Theology,* I, p. 189.
13. *Ibid.,* p. 201.
14. *Ibid.,* pp. 190–191.

belongs. Thus infinity is not the negation of finitude as such, but the overcoming of the negative element in finitude, the power of nonbeing.

The potential presence of the infinite (as unlimited self-transcendence) is the negation of the negative element in finitude. It is the negation of nonbeing.[15]

We have established thus far that in Tillich's thought there is no contrast between finite beings and an infinite being. If there were such a contrast, reunion of the two could not be viewed as self-reconciliation. Rather, for Tillich, finitude and infinity are realities related in a polar fashion. Finitude aware of itself requires infinity; infinity is nothing more than the transcendence of finitude. By losing his true or essential finitude, man has also lost his participation in infinity, as the infinite transcendence of finitude. As with the other polar elements, to lose the one is to lose the other.

As we have seen, the power of self-transcendence is, according to Tillich, a manifestation of the power of being-itself. Being-itself, however, cannot, strictly speaking, be identified with infinity, even understood as the power of transcending finitude. In Tillich's view, being-itself transcends the polarity of finitude and its transcendence.

Being-itself is not infinity; it is that which lies beyond the polarity of finitude and infinite self-transcendence. . . . It precedes the finite, and it precedes the infinite negation of the finite.[16]

Thus unity with being-itself does not involve simply the overcoming of finitude; finitude is both posited and overcome within the ground of being. This conclusion, that man combines finitude and infinity, is an important aspect of Tillich's case against naturalism and pantheism.

Another aspect of finitude must be described in its relation to being-itself. This might be called the affective dimension of finitude. Finitude in experience, according to Tillich, becomes

15. *Ibid.*, p. 191.
16. *Ibid.*

anxiety. Anxiety, as the inward reaction to the threat of non-being, must be overcome with a quality of self-affirmation which Tillich calls "courage."

> Courage is the self-affirmation of being in spite of the fact of non-being. It is the act of the individual self in taking the anxiety of nonbeing upon itself.[17]

Thus courage is an affect, but it has an ontological root. It is a power of being.

No aspect of man's finite being can provide or sustain this kind of courage. This is true, Tillich maintains, of man's finite participation as well as of his finite individuality. One can no more derive ultimate self-affirmation from participation—whether it be biological, psychological, or sociological—than he can from himself in his solitude. It is true that a part of man's being is participation in his world (what Tillich calls "being as a part"), but this too is subject to threat. Tillich states:

> But being as a part points to the fact that self-affirmation necessarily includes the affirmation of oneself as "participant," and that this side of our self-affirmation is threatened by nonbeing as much as the other side, the affirmation of the self as an individual self. We are threatened not only with losing our individual selves but also with losing participation in our world. Therefore self-affirmation as a part requires courage as much as does self-affirmation as oneself. It is *one* courage which takes a double threat of nonbeing into itself.[18]

This point has a bearing on the critique of Fromm from Tillich's viewpoint. Fromm seems to derive the "courage to be," what he calls "productivity," from man's participation in nature. Tillich is saying here that man does participate in various finite structures, but because it is finite all such participation is subject to threat and cannot sustain itself.

The source of ultimate courage or self-affirmation must be beyond finitude and the threat of nonbeing altogether. It must derive from the ground of being.

17. Tillich, *The Courage to Be*, p. 155.
18. *Ibid.*, p. 89.

Courage needs the power of being, a power transcending the non-being which is experienced in the anxiety of fate and death, which is present in the anxiety of emptiness and meaninglessness, which is effective in the anxiety of guilt and condemnation. The courage which takes this threefold anxiety into itself must be rooted in a power of being that is greater than the power of oneself and the power of one's world.[19]

Wherever a source for such courage is described it becomes, in Tillich's view, a symbol for being-itself, though in secular form. According to this line of thought, Fromm's concept of "productivity" would be a symbol for the power of being-itself. Thus Tillich's view is that productivity or courage cannot be derived from nature because nature is finite and subject to the threat of nonbeing. Fromm, on the other hand, seems to view nature as self-sufficient and infinite.

Our discussion of anxiety and courage, then, results in a description of another aspect of the unity of finitude with being-itself. It is in being-itself that a source is found for the self-affirmation which can withstand the threat of nonbeing. Here again, as in our analysis of self-transcendence, the union with being-itself is not a unity with an alien being but an augmentation of the self and its "courage to be."

In Tillich's analysis, furthermore, courage or self-affirmation and self-transcendence have closely related meanings. In *The Courage to Be,* Tillich suggests that "vitality" (which he earlier equates with courage and self-affirmation) is the power of a being to transcend itself.

[Man] can transcend any given situation in any direction and this possibility drives him to create beyond himself. Vitality is the power of creating beyond oneself without losing oneself.[20]

If self-affirmation and self-transcendence are rooted in the power of being-itself, we must take one further step. The possibility of self-contradiction, based upon man's ability to "go out

19. *Ibid.,* p. 155.
20. *Ibid.,* p. 81.

from" himself, must also be rooted in the power of being-itself. Self-transcendence may become self-contradiction. When Tillich discusses the possibility of self-contradiction, he normally connects it with finite freedom. The characteristics of finite freedom in Tillich's analysis, however, would seem to be identical in most respects with the characteristics of self-transcendence. According to Tillich's own statement, self-transcendence is "the first and basic quality of freedom."[21] Thus it would seem legitimate to relate self-contradiction to self-transcendence.

When Tillich states that "reality itself moves through 'yes' and 'no,' through positive, negative, and positive again," he seems to mean more than self-transcendence. Reality not only goes out of itself; it also contradicts itself. Speaking of the dependence of man upon the ground of being, and his independence of it, Tillich writes:

Man actualizes his finite freedom in unity with the whole of reality. This actualization includes structural independence, the power of standing upon one's self, and the possibility of resisting the return to the ground of being. . . . Creaturely existence includes a double resistance, that is, resistance against nonbeing as well as resistance against the ground of being in which it is rooted and upon which it is dependent.[22]

If our analysis is correct, this resistance against the ground of being is a kind of self-contradiction which yet is rooted in the ground of being. This analysis points up again the ambiguous characteristics of self-transcendence (and hence of life) in Tillich's thought which were referred to in previous chapters. This ambiguity may in turn be rooted in the duality of Tillich's attitude toward nonbeing. It is nonbeing which forces being to affirm itself, and hence to transcend itself. In more graphic terms, life cannot be life without death. Is Tillich saying that life must in a sense go into and through death before it can emerge

21. Tillich, *Systematic Theology*, III, p. 303; compare "self-transcendence," Tillich, *Systematic Theology*, I, pp. 181–182, with "freedom," Tillich, *Systematic Theology*, II, pp. 31–32.
22. Tillich, *Systematic Theology*, I, p. 261.

victorious? This might explain the ambiguity of self-transcendence. This may, in fact, be Tillich's version of the Christian (and Hegelian) theme of life through death.

It is participation in being-itself, then, which gives to finite being the characteristics of self-affirmation, self-transcendence, and the possibility of self-contradiction. These three traits, as we have seen in Chapter Eight, can be described as characteristics of "life," in Tillich's view. We reach the conclusion, then, that it is life which is given to finite being by its participation in being-itself—life which has as its characteristics the movement from potentiality toward actuality, through self-affirmation and self-transcendence, along with the possibility of self-contradiction. Essential man, man in unity with being-itself, possesses life, life affirmed, and the threat of nonbeing overcome.

Thus finitude, in dialectical polarity with infinitude, is sustained by its participation in the power of being. Rather than being negated by its union with being-itself, finitude is able to affirm itself in the power of being. Union with God is not unity with an alien being but with the power of one's own life. Further clarification of the relation between God and his creatures requires that we combine Tillich's analysis of the Christian symbols with his analysis of finitude.

tillich's
theological answers:
part two

The Christian Symbols and
their Demythologization   W<small>E ARE</small> now in a position to combine Tillich's analysis of the Christian symbols
(creation and fall) and his "halfway demythologization" (the
movement from essence to existence) with his analysis of finitude
in its relation to infinity and to being-itself. Only by combining
these two analyses can we gain an accurate picture of the relation
between God and the creation in Tillich's thought, and thus
evaluate his interpretation of the Christian doctrines of creation
and fall.

As we have seen, Tillich holds that there is an eternal unity
between God and man, between finitude and being-itself, within
the divine life. This essential finitude within God is the product
of God's "internal creativity." Always speaking symbolically,
Tillich maintains that essential finitude has its being in an eternal
process of separation and reunion within the divine life.[1] God as
the living God is eternally creative within himself. Thus it would
seem clear that for Tillich this separation and individualization
going on within the divine life is a form of eternal creation.

If finitude is thus present "within the divine life," this means
that the threat of nonbeing is also present. In essential finitude,
according to Tillich, this threat is continually being overcome by
the power of being.

1. Tillich, *Systematic Theology,* I, p. 282.

144

God as creative life includes the finite and, with it, nonbeing, although nonbeing is eternally conquered and the finite is eternally reunited within the infinity of the divine life.[2]

And if this is true of finitude, then the "forms of finitude" (for example, space and time) are present also, though they are at the same time transcended. All of this suggests that for Tillich the essential characteristics of finitude—individualization and separateness (in polar relation to participation), the threat of nonbeing, spatiality, temporality—belong to the "original" good creation, and are not, as such, a mark of man's fallenness.

This view is implied specifically in Tillich's distinction between two types of separation.

Separation can mean individualization; in this sense it is an element in the structure of being and is rooted in the divine life: it is one condition of love—the other being reunion. Separation as individualization is good, it is the presupposition of all actual goodness. But separation is also used for the estrangement and conflict between God and man, between man and man, and even within man. Taken in this sense, separation is sin and reunion is salvation.[3]

If our interpretation is correct, the first type of separation referred to here exists within the unity of the divine life. This view is also implied in Tillich's concept of "essential solitude." If, then, the characteristics of finitude (and especially man's separateness) belong to an original good creation, they will not be negated in the process of salvation or reunion. As our analysis proceeds, however, we shall have to ask to what extent individualization can be complete within the divine life.

If Tillich's concept of creation were to stop at this point, it could accurately be described as a pantheistic, rather than a Christian, formulation. The creation, though individualized, has its being within the womb of the divine, not independently of the divine. Separation is to be understood within the context of a broader unity. This view would, in fact, approximate the naturalistic

2. *Ibid.*, p. 270.
3. Tillich, "Reply," in *The Theology of Paul Tillich*, ed. by Kegley and Bretall, p. 344.

understanding of separation from nature as only partial (i.e., in consciousness), and of salvation as a rediscovery of man's actual oneness with nature or the universe.

Tillich's account of creation, however, does not terminate with the concept of essential finitude within the divine life. In his view, the creation remains incomplete until it has been fulfilled through the realization of "finite freedom." According to Tillich, it is the actuality of finite freedom which makes pantheism impossible.

It is the quality of finite freedom within the created which makes pantheism impossible and not the notion of a highest being alongside the world, whether his relation to the world is described in deistic or theistic terms.[4]

The creation must be viewed as "outside" the divine life because it contains the quality of finite freedom.

The creature has actualized its freedom insofar as it is outside the creative ground of the divine life. This is the difference between being inside and outside the divine life. "Inside" and "outside" are spatial symbols, but what they say is not spatial. They refer to something qualitative rather than quantitative. To be outside the divine life means to stand in actualized freedom, in an existence which is no longer united with essence.[5]

The realization of freedom, then, according to Tillich, involves a form of separation which would appear to be distinct from the separation of individualization. We must now examine the nature of this separation to determine, on the one hand, its relation to individualization, and, on the other hand, its relation to estrangement. If it is really equivalent to the individualization within the divine life, the creation remains a movement within essential being, and the transition to existence becomes inexplicable; but if it is equivalent to estrangement, then the completion of the creation and the fall necessarily coincide.

We have suggested above that Tillich's concept of freedom is closely related to his concept of self-transcendence. We can now

4. Tillich, *Systematic Theology*, II, p. 8.
5. Tillich, *Systematic Theology*, I, p. 255.

clarify this assertion by suggesting that self-transcendence is the element of separation in finite freedom. Descriptive accounts of these two concepts in the *Systematic Theology* indicate that they overlap in many, though perhaps not in every, respect. Tillich describes self-transcendence in the following fashion:

[Man] can transcend himself without limits in all directions. . . . His creativity breaks through the biological realm to which he belongs and establishes new realms never attainable on a nonhuman level. Man is able to create a new world of technical tools and a world of cultural forms. In both cases something new comes into being through man's grasping and shaping activity. Man uses the material given by nature to create technical forms which transcend nature, and he creates cultural forms which have validity and meaning. Living in these forms, he transforms himself, while originating them. . . . His self-transcendence in this direction is indefinite, while the biological self-transcendence has reached its limits in him.[6]

In summarizing the characteristics of finite freedom, Tillich writes:

Man is free, in so far as he has language. . . . Man is free, in so far as he is able to ask questions about the world he encounters, including himself. . . . Man is free, in so far as he can receive unconditional moral and logical imperatives which indicate that he can transcend the conditions which determine every finite being. Man is free, in so far as he has the power of deliberating and deciding, thus cutting through the mechanisms of stimulus and response. Man is free, in so far as he can play and build imaginary structures above the real structures to which he, like all beings is bound. Man is free, in so far as he has the faculty of creating worlds above the given world, of creating the world of technical tools and products, the world of artistic expressions, the world of theoretical structures and practical organizations. Finally, man is free, in so far as he has the power of contradicting himself and his essential nature. Man is free even from his freedom.[7]

These two passages suggest that for Tillich freedom and self-transcendence mutually involve each other and overlap considerably in meaning. The idea of going out from oneself in creativity is to be seen in each formulation.

6. *Ibid.*, pp. 181–182.
7. Tillich, *Systematic Theology*, II, pp. 31–32.

Elsewhere, Tillich also indicates that freedom and self-transcendence are closely related in meaning. He writes:

Freedom is the possibility of transcending a given situation. Man is free, for instance, from history in so far as he knows history, thus transcending the immediate temporal process by which he is driven from the past to the future. Man is free from his own necessity in so far as he knows it and is, in this respect, not *in* it.[8]

Again, he writes that man's freedom expresses itself in four ways as follows:

... first the freedom of transcending any given situation and of imagining and realizing something new.... in the second place ... transcending himself in the direction of complete universality and individuality.... third ... creating with purpose.... fourth ... freedom from-one's-own-freedom or the freedom to play with one's world and one's self.[9]

Finally, Tillich indicates that self-transcendence is "the first and basic quality of freedom."[10]

We have documented this relationship in some detail because it is quite significant for our entire analysis. We conclude that when Tillich attributes the possibility of the "transition from essence to existence" to finite freedom, he is referring to the ability of man to go out from his own essence in self-transcendence. The separation involved in this transition is a separation based upon self-transcendence. If this distinction is to be maintained, however, we must show that completed self-transcendence is a form of separation distinguishable from the separation of individualization. We shall seek to show that for Tillich the *completion* or *final culmination* of individualization requires the separation of self-transcendence, and that it is the latter separation, and not the former in incomplete stages, which carries the creation "outside" the divine life.

8. Tillich, "Man and Society in Religious Socialism," *Christianity and Society*, VIII (Fall, 1943), p. 14.

9. Tillich, "The Conception of Man in Existential Philosophy," *Journal of Religion*, 19 (July, 1939), No. 3, pp. 206–208.

10. Tillich, *Systematic Theology*, III, p. 303.

According to Tillich, individualization is a characteristic of all real beings. "Individualization is not a characteristic of a special sphere of beings; it is an ontological element and therefore a *quality* of everything."[11] He follows Aristotle in viewing individualization as the *"telos,* the inner aim, of the process of actualization."[12] An essential aspect of individuality, according to Tillich, is self-relatedness or self-centeredness. By these terms he seems to mean a structured whole, an organization of parts, or an organism.

The very term "individual" points to the interdependence of self-relatedness and individualization. A self-centered being cannot be divided. It can be destroyed, or it can be deprived of certain parts out of which new self-centered beings emerge (e.g., regeneration of structure in some lower animals). In the latter case either the old self has ceased to exist and is replaced by new selves or the old self remains, diminished in extension and power for the sake of the new selves. But in no case is the center itself divided.[13]

The process of individualization and of self-relatedness is completed in the achievement of selfhood. "Every self is self-related and a complete self is completely self-related. It is an independent *centre,* indivisible and impenetrable, and therefore rightly called an individual."[14] In terms of the characteristic of self-centeredness, it is possible to speak of a degree of selfhood in living beings other than man, and by analogy in inanimate things.

Selfhood or self-centeredness must be attributed in some measure to all living beings and, in terms of analogy, to all individual *Gestalten* even in the inorganic realm.[15]

At times Tillich seems to apply the term "self" to those beings which have some form of consciousness of being separate from,

11. Tillich, *Systematic Theology,* I, pp. 174–175.
12. *Ibid.,* p. 174; cf. Tillich, "Being and Love," in *Moral Principles of Action,* ed. by Ruth N. Anshen, p. 663, where he states that "being drives toward individualization."
13. Tillich, *Systematic Theology,* I, p. 175; Tillich seems to use self-centeredness and self-relatedness synonymously; the process of actualizing centeredness Tillich terms "self-integration," and he identifies this process in *Systematic Theology,* III, as one of the basic functions of life.
14. Tillich, *Love, Power, and Justice,* pp. 25–26.
15. Tillich, *Systematic Theology,* I, p. 169.

and participating in, an environment. In this context, he distinguishes between a "self" and an "ego-self," apparently distinguishing between animal consciousness and human consciousness. But again Tillich finds an analogy on the levels of being below consciousness. Every being "has" an environment which it is "in," and with which it is interrelated. Indeed, Tillich holds that all beings share in the self-world polarity, though approximating more or less closely to one of the poles.

> Metaphysical theories as well as social institutions in which selves are transformed into things contradict truth and justice, for they contradict the basic ontological structure of being, the self-world polarity in which every being participates in varying degrees of approximation to the one or the other pole.[16]

Tillich sees, then, a progressive development of individualization, self-centeredness, and selfhood in nature, culminating in man. Animal consciousness would seem to be an important step in this progression, but it too is incomplete. Man has self-consciousness. We might infer from Tillich's usage that whereas consciousness has its own body as its object, self-consciousness has the power of turning about and viewing itself as subject-self as object. "But man can oppose his self to every part of his world, including himself as a part of his world."[17] We might say that an ego-self is a self aware of itself-aware-of-its-world. This view seems to be implied in the following statement:

> When man looks at his world, he looks at himself as an infinitely small part of his world. Although he is the perspective-center, he becomes a particle of what is centered in him, a particle of the universe. This structure enables man to encounter himself. Without its world the self would be an empty form. Self-consciousness would have no content, for every content, psychic as well as bodily, lies within the universe.[18]

The psychic content referred to must include the subject-self as object, as well as other subject-selves. This consciousness of

16. *Ibid.,* p. 173.
17. Tillich, *Systematic Theology,* III, p. 39.
18. Tillich, *Systematic Theology,* I, p. 171.

subject-self as object is necessary for full world consciousness.

Self-consciousness, then, viewed from one perspective, is the completion of world consciousness and, correlatively, of individualization and self-relatedness. Individualization is inseparable from participation, which here takes the form of world consciousness or awareness. The separation involved in individualization thus is also completed in the realization of self-consciousness, which is separation from every content, including the subject-self; but thus far separation has been viewed in correlation with participation, that is, with world consciousness.

This self-consciousness which completes individualization, however, involves a new form of separation. Self-consciousness is inseparable from self-transcendence. Tillich's usage here is highly complex. In one sense, all beings transcend themselves in that they all move toward new forms. "The dynamic character of being implies the tendency of everything to transcend itself and to create new forms."[19] Viewed in this context, self-transcendence is simply incomplete and limited on the subhuman levels.

Just as the self on the subhuman level is imperfect and in correlation with an environment, while on the human level the self is perfect and in correlation with a world, so self-transcendence on the subhuman level is limited by a constellation of conditions, while self-transcendence on the human level is limited only by the structure which makes man what he is—a complete self which has a world.[20]

Man, however, experiences, or is aware of, self-transcendence in himself. "Self-transcendence and self-conservation are experienced immediately by man in man himself."[21] This formulation suggests that man's self-awareness is not as such ontologically equivalent to self-transcendence; it is simply the conscious experience of it. Tillich, speaking of the "reflection" of self-transcendence in consciousness, writes: "Man is the mirror in which the

19. *Ibid.*, p. 181.
20. *Ibid.*
21. *Ibid.*

relation of everything finite to the infinite becomes conscious."[22] According to this line of thought, self-consciousness arises when full self-transcendence is achieved ontologically. Yet self-consciousness is the aspect of self-transcendence which man knows from within. The knowledge of self-transcendence necessarily accompanies the reality. Here as elsewhere for Tillich psychology is the key to ontology cognitively, though it is not identical with it. Tillich does not seem to view self-consciousness as an additional dimension of self-transcendence so much as an accompaniment of its full realization, though a necessary one. The awareness of self-transcendence, moreover, makes man aware of his finitude and indicates that he possesses a potential infinity. Here again self-consciousness does not constitute this potential infinity but makes man aware of it. Insofar as all beings transcend themselves, they also possess a potential infinity; but man is the only being aware of his finiteness and his potential infinity.

The achievement of complete self-transcendence, however, as we have suggested, results in a new type of separation. The self separates itself from its world (and its own body) in order to be reunited with it through consciousness. The content of the self is limited by the world. The ego-self, or the self which separates itself from itself, however (and this completes the separation from the world), takes a perspective which is beyond the world altogether and is therefore inherently unlimited. Man through self-transcendence (or what Tillich here calls "dynamics") reaches beyond nature and creates a world of his own.

Man is able to create a world beyond the given world; he creates the technical and spiritual realms. The dynamics of subhuman life remain within the limits of natural necessity, notwithstanding the infinite variations it produces and notwithstanding the new forms created by the evolutionary process. Dynamics reaches out beyond nature only in man.[23]

The point of transition between finitude within the divine life

22. Tillich, *Systematic Theology,* III, p. 87.
23. Tillich, *Systematic Theology,* I, p. 180.

and finite freedom outside the divine life, according to Tillich, is the advent of consciousness of potential freedom (and self-transcendence) and the desire to actualize it. If our analysis is correct, this awareness is the experienced aspect of a certain degree of self-transcendence. Any greater degree of self-transcendence requires that the being stand outside itself and thus at the same time outside the divine life. This degree of ontological self-transcendence arouses self-consciousness and, more specifically, anxiety; the transcendence of finitude creates awareness of finitude. The fullest degree of self-transcendence must be accepted and affirmed consciously by man in order to become actual.

It is possible to ask: Would this degree of self-transcendence without self-consciousness become separated from the divine life? Does self-consciousness actually effect the transition from essence to existence? On the basis of our analysis it would seem that this question cannot be answered, since this degree of self-transcendence inevitably involves self-consciousness. But the two movements can be distinguished: self-transcendence is an ontological movement, self-consciousness is its "mirror."[24] As we shall see, Tillich insists that the separation necessitates an act of freedom. It is here that ontology and psychology coincide: freedom is self-transcendence, an ontological reality; but it is also self-consciousness, a psychological reality. (It might be noted that Tillich has thus made, not only God's internal creativity, but also the external creation eternal. As our analysis has shown, being drives inevitably toward the fullest individualization which includes the fullest self-transcendence.)

It is man's freedom, self-transcendence, self-consciousness, and creativity which carries the creation "outside" the divine life. The realization of these elements therefore completes the creation. It is this separation, moreover, which becomes estrangement. We must ask at this point whether this form of separation *must* be-

24. Tillich, *Systematic Theology*, III, p. 87.

come estrangement, according to Tillich's analysis. This involves a further examination of freedom and self-transcendence.

Freedom and Estrangement

As we concluded earlier, the realm of self-transcendence is the realm of freedom from "natural necessity." Man is free to choose the goals of his creativity. There is a sense in which man is free from himself as well as from the given world. On the basis of his own nature he is free from his own nature. Yet freedom can sustain itself, according to Tillich, only if in its freedom it chooses that which is in keeping with its own nature.

For freedom can maintain itself only insofar as it chooses the content, the norms and the values in which our essential nature, including our freedom, expresses itself.[25]

Again, describing man's dynamics (which in this passage again is seemingly equivalent to self-transcendence), Tillich writes:

Man's dynamics, his creative vitality, is not undirected, chaotic, self-contained activity. It is directed, formed; it transcends itself toward meaningful contents.[26]

Significantly for this discussion, Tillich at one point indicates that in man's essential nature there are forms even for the transcendence of form.

Every living being (and, in terms of analogy, every being) drives beyond itself and beyond the given form through which it has being. In man's essential nature, dynamics and form are united. Even if a given form is transcended, this happens in terms of form. In essential being there are forms of the self-transcendence of form. Their unity with the dynamics of being is never disrupted.[27]

In the state of potentiality (or essentiality), dynamics and form are in harmony, though neither is actualized, just as freedom and destiny are in harmony before actualization. Tillich elsewhere describes man's essential self-transcendence in this way:

    25. Tillich, "The Conception of Man in Existentialist Philosophy," p. 208.
    26. Tillich, *Systematic Theology*, I, pp. 180–181.
    27. Tillich, *Systematic Theology*, II, p. 64.

We can imagine a finiteness which is continuously overcome and conserved by our infinity. We have experiences of a transitoriness which does not defy our eternity but is an element in it. We know a feeling in which the very fact that we are able to face our nothingness includes the certainty that we are beyond it.[28]

The importance of this formulation for our purposes is that a being may transcend itself without losing or contradicting itself. If a being has the potentiality for transcending itself without losing itself (or its form), it would seem that this would be a genuine possibility within actuality. Is it not meaningless to say that there is a potentiality which cannot become actuality? Is it not then *possible* for man to become separate from his essence (and the divine life) without becoming estranged?

At times Tillich seems to speak as though self-contradiction were only a possibility of freedom and self-transcendence. Thus he states: "The ability to transcend any given situation implies the possibility of losing oneself in the infinity of transcending oneself."[29] Certain later statements tend to suggest the same view of estrangement as a possibility of freedom. Thus Tillich states:

Finally, man is free, in so far as he has the power of contradicting himself and his essential nature. Man is free even from his freedom; that is, he can surrender his humanity.[30]

Or again:

Man also has an environment, but he has it as a part of his world. He can and does transcend it with every word he speaks. He is free to make his world into an object which he beholds, and he is free to make himself into an object upon which he looks. In this situation of finite freedom he can lose himself and his world, and the loss of one necessarily includes the loss of the other.[31]

In these statements, estrangement would appear to be a possibility, rather than a necessity, of freedom. In other words, estrange-

28. Tillich, "The Conception of Man in Existentialist Philosophy," p. 210.
29. *Ibid.,* p. 208.
30. Tillich, *Systematic Theology,* II, p. 32.
31. *Ibid.,* p. 60.

ment arises from a certain type of free choice, rather than from the act of free choice. Though the term "self-transcendence" is itself ambiguous, it would not seem, in Tillich's usage, to carry inherently the meaning of self-contradiction.

The prevailing theme of Tillich's analysis at this point, however, is that estrangement inevitably accompanies the actualization of freedom. Tillich's strongest statement to this effect is found in *Love, Power, and Justice:*

Actualization of one's potentialities includes, unavoidably, estrangement; estrangement from one's essential being, so that we may find it again in maturity.[32]

In a similar fashion he describes the realization of unambiguous life:

Therefore, the creation of unambiguous life brings about the reunion of these elements in life processes in which actual being is the true expression of potential being, an expression, however, which is not immediate, as in "dreaming innocence," but which is realized only after estrangement, contest, and decision.[33]

According to this view, the separation involved in actualizing freedom, thus completing the creation, *is* estrangement. Thus the completion of creation and the fall coincide.

Being a creature means both to be rooted in the creative ground of the divine life and to actualize one's self through freedom. Creation is fulfilled in the creaturely self-realization which simultaneously is freedom and destiny. But it is fulfilled through separation from the creative ground through a break between existence and essence. Creaturely freedom is the point at which creation and the fall coincide.[34]

Self-realization involves the loss of unity with the ground of being and one's essential nature; and Tillich states that "the actualization of finite freedom means tragedy, the curse over man and his

32. Tillich, *Love, Power, and Justice,* p. 112; it is here that Tillich sounds most like Hegel and Fromm.
33. Tillich, *Systematic Theology,* III, p. 129.
34. Tillich, *Systematic Theology,* I, p. 256.

world."[35] It is probable that this formulation is more in keeping with Tillich's over-all system, as outlined in the previous chapter. The actualization of freedom, or self-transcendence, is viewed primarily as an ontological movement of separation; and this separation is estrangement. Therefore the completion of the creation inevitably involves estrangement.

This conclusion is not affected by Tillich's assertion that the fall is not a "structural necessity." He insists that the actualization of freedom and the fall is fact, but not necessity.

Creation is good in its essential character. If actualized it falls into universal estrangement through freedom and destiny. The hesitation of many critics to accept these obviously realistic statements is caused by their justified fear that sin may become a rational necessity, as in purely essentialist systems. Against them theology must insist that the leap from essence to existence is the original fact— that it has the character of a leap and not of structural necessity. In spite of its tragic universality, existence cannot be derived from essence.[36]

We must be careful to understand what Tillich is saying here. The essences are for Tillich the rational structure of the universe. They represent the structural requirements or necessities of a possible universe. But there is nothing in the essences which requires such a universe to exist. One cannot derive the existent universe from an analysis of the essences. Therefore, in this sense, existence is fact and not rational necessity. The final act of creation (as we shall see, an act of God and man) is a free act, not a rational necessity.

There is, however, another kind of necessity. If the creation is to be completed, it must become estranged. This assertion involves, to be sure, a concept of the completed creation and of God's nature. These topics will be discussed in the next section. However, we may say here that if freedom is to be actualized, the creation must become estranged. There is no structural requirement for man to actualize his freedom; therefore it is not necessary

35. Tillich, "Man and Society in Religious Socialism," p. 14.
36. Tillich, *Systematic Theology,* II, p. 44.

that he become estranged. But if man is to actualize his freedom, then it is necessary that he become estranged. Further, if our earlier analysis of Tillich's conception of creation is correct, it is viewed as eternal, since being drives toward individualization. This same drive would then impel being inevitably to become self-estranged. Estrangement is necessary to complete individualization. It would appear that in these senses the fall is eternalized and made necessary in Tillich's system. It is a necessity of life, not of logic.

Two further comments concerning this formulation of the doctrines of creation and fall might be made at this point. First, with regard to the creation, it would seem clear that for Tillich man completes his own creation. Human freedom is the means by which God completes the creation, rather than the final product of God's creation. Thus the creative act which alienates is a human act rather than a divine act (though as we shall see below, human freedom is the divine freedom). The point suggested previously that Tillich views human creativity as tragic might be recalled here. This theme in Tillich is reminiscent of the Marxian theme that man creates the world in which he lives.

Secondly, the tragic nature of human freedom raises a question about the freedom of Jesus, the Christ, bearer of the New Being. Jesus, being truly human and therefore in actualized freedom, would have to become estranged, according to Tillich's formulation, before he could be reconciled. This approach could lead to an adoptionist Christology, rather than to the traditional Chalcedonian doctrine. Here Jesus would not be the Christ until reconciled in maturity. Only if Tillich conceded the possibility of freedom without estrangement could the estrangement of Jesus the Christ be avoided. Otherwise, Tillich's insistence upon the universality of estrangement must be followed to its logical conclusion.

We have now completed our examination of Tillich's concepts of creation and fall, or of essential finitude and existential estrangement, insofar as these are viewed from the point of view of man. We discovered that man's estrangement from essential finitude is, in fact, an estrangement from God or being-itself. If estrangement is self-estrangement, however, it should be possible to speak of God as self-estranged also. We now turn to a consideration of self-estrangement and self-reconciliation from the point of view of the divine self-estrangement.

Divine Self-Estrangement and Self-Reconciliation

According to Tillich, one of the most salient points of Biblical religion is its understanding of God as a living God. We have shown that in order to attribute life to God, Tillich holds it necessary to distinguish between the ambiguous life of finite existence and the unambiguous life of God. With this qualification, the concept of life is an acceptable symbol for the divine reality. As we have seen, the concept of life for Tillich contains the ideas of creativity and self-transcendence. God is creative and self-transcendent because he is living. Also, if our analysis of Tillich's meaning is correct, the divine life, self-transcendence, and creativity are manifest in human life, self-transcendence, and creativity. The act by which God "goes out from himself" in self-transcendence and creativity is the same act by which the creature affirms his independence of his ground.

The self-transcendent idea of God replaces the spatial imagery—at least for theological thought—by the concept of finite freedom. The divine transcendence is identical with the freedom of the created to turn away from the essenital unity with the creative ground of its being.[37]

This understanding of self-transcendence and creativity gives a basis for Tillich's assertion that there is a point at which creation and the fall coincide. Human creativity, or self-transcendence, is both a manifestation of the divine life and a "departure" from it. By an extension of this reasoning, we may say that human self-estrangement is also divine self-estrangement. If the created order is the divine life going out from itself, when the creation

37. *Ibid.*, p. 8.

becomes estranged, God becomes estranged as well. Tillich at
one point suggests that we can speak of God as self-estranged, at
least symbolically.[38]

When we compare the meaning of self-estrangement for God
with its meaning for man, however, certain differences emerge.
Man's estrangement is at the same time the completion of the
creation and the beginning of the fall. As the fall of man, estrangement combines individual sin and tragic destiny. As an act involving human freedom, it is not structurally necessary. Viewed from
the perspective of God, however, insofar as this can be done
symbolically, it would seem that self-estrangement is a necessary
step in the actualization of the divine nature (with a qualification
to be mentioned). It would seem that estrangement is necessary,
in Tillich's view, for the full realization of the divine life, fulfilled
as love.

The Christian tradition affirms that God is love. Tillich understands love in all its forms as the drive toward the reunion of the
separated.[39] For love to be actual, then, there must be genuine
separation. As Tillich puts it:

Love is real only if there is a "serious otherness," as Hegel has
called it. But in the trinitarian process, going on between Father and
Son in the medium of the Spirit, is no serious otherness. Therefore
it is a play of the divine with itself, playing love, but not serious
love. In less romantic terms this means that the ground of being is
the principle of Love but that Love is actual or serious only in relation to the beings. For the beings are separated from their Ground
by their freedom.[40]

Thus, according to Tillich, it is in the very nature of the ground
of being to go out from itself in individualization, in order to overcome separation and return to itself as love.

---

38. Tillich, "Estrangement and Reconciliation in Modern Thought,"
p. 6.
39. Tillich, Systematic Theology, II, p. 47; cf. Tillich, Love, Power,
and Justice, p. 28.
40. Tillich, "Being and Love," in Moral Principles of Action, p. 663.

The answer to the question "what does it mean that God is Love,"
is this: the ground of being from which every being takes its power
of being has the character of self-separating and self-returning life.
Self-separating is the abbreviation for complete individualization.
Self-returning is the abbreviation of the return of life to itself in the
power of reuniting love.[41]

It is possible to speak of God loving himself in terms of the trinitarian distinctions and in terms of loving the finite potentialities
within the divine life. But God's self-love is incomplete until it is
fulfilled in terms of loving the free creatures outside the divine life.

The divine life is the divine self-love. Through the separation *within*
himself God loves himself. And through separation *from* himself
(in creaturely freedom) God fulfils his love of himself—primarily
because he loves that which is estranged from himself.[42]

We have previously noted that, according to Tillich, being drives
toward the most complete separation, or individualization. We
have also noted his view that the greatest achievement of individuality occurs in the realization of selfhood, or self-centeredness.
This drive of being toward the greatest separation is a necessary
movement with regard to the completion of love. It is the fulfillment and the triumph of love to be able to reunite the most separate beings.

Love reunites that which is self-centered and individual. The power
of love is not something which is added to an otherwise finished
process, but life has love in itself as one of its constituitive elements.
It is the fulfillment and the triumph of love that it is able to reunite
the most radically separated beings, namely individual persons.[43]

Thus separation is essential to the fulfillment of love.

The separation of individual beings is overcome through their
reunion with the ground of being. The communion of those who
possess solitude is rooted in the relation to the ground of being.

41. *Ibid.*, p. 671.
42. Tillich, *Systematic Theology*, I, p. 282.
43. Tillich, *Love, Power, and Justice*, p. 26.

In solitude man experiences the dimension of the ultimate, the true basis for communion among those who are alone.[44]

Love overcomes separation without destroying individuality. As Tillich puts it: "The difference actualizes the identity and transforms identity into Love."[45] Leibrecht interprets this aspect of Tillich's thought as follows:

Since being is love, it drives toward individualization. It is love which makes being the power of creation, but the essential identity in the ground of being is not disrupted or denied by this element of "serious otherness." For Tillich shows that the very identity of the ultimate Ground is possible only through difference.[46]

For Tillich, then, the divine love is fulfilled through love for the creatures who are estranged. This separation, or estrangement, as we have seen, presupposes a more basic oneness, or unity. Therefore it is possible to say that God's love for the world is in a real sense his own self-love. This assertion should not be taken, however, as a minimization of the individuality of the creatures. The divine justice preserves individuality, even in reunion.

It might be fair, then, to summarize Tillich's view of love as the discovery of identity in difference, of self in other. This is true even for Tillich's account of *agapé*. This form of love does indeed seek "fulfillment of the other"; it "accepts the other in spite of resistance." Thus God's *agapé* "works toward the fulfillment of every creature."[47] *Agapé* is concerned with the other being, but this is the case because *agapé* seeks the fulfillment of the whole; it sees the unity of the whole through its separation. *Agapé* "seeks the other because of the ultimate unity of being with being within the divine ground."[48] Tillich speaks of the ultimate unity as love seeking love; but, recalling the close relation of love to life for

44. Tillich, *Systematic Theology*, II, p. 71.
45. Tillich, "Being and Love," in *Moral Principles of Action*, p. 663.
46. Walter Leibrecht, "The Life and Mind of Paul Tillich," in *Religion and Culture*, ed. by Walter Leibrecht, p. 25.
47. Tillich, *Systematic Theology*, I, pp. 280–281.
48. *Ibid.*

Tillich, we see that his formulation here is close to that of the early Hegel; through love, life in the subject senses life in the object. Tillich's treatment of love indicates that for him all estrangement can finally be viewed as a form of self-estrangement.

We noted earlier that Fromm seeks to combine a concept of love as desire for reunion with one of mature love as overflowing abundance or vitality. We also noted that this combination results in an unresolved tension in his formulation. Tillich recommends viewing all love as having a fundamental ontological unity, but with different qualities. As we have seen, the vitality of life for Tillich stems from separation and the drive toward reunion. Life is destroyed if either is eliminated; separation and reunion are united in life. Tillich thus unifies the concepts of love into a consistent whole, but has he not done so by incorporating the *agapé* motif as a subordinate theme within the *erōs* motif?[49] Is this not a victory of a Greek motif over a Christian one?

We might summarize the results of our analysis. In Tillich's view, God as life contains within himself finitude and its transcendence, subjectivity and objectivity, the threat of nonbeing and its continual negation. However, to realize himself fully as life (fulfilled as love), God cannot rest in his inner creativity and self-transcendence but must go out from himself in actual self-transcendence and freedom, allowing finitude to stand upon itself. This creation, which goes out from the divine nature, is itself life, combining the same characteristics, but now subject to disruption. The fulfillment of life, human and divine, occurs when life returns enriched to itself through love. Tillich has discovered, as he believes, a framework within which the world can be viewed as a part of the divine life, yet endowed with independence and freedom. The power of all life is the power of being; but in affirming themselves through this power, beings become alienated from being-itself. Alienated beings cannot in their own power return to unity with the Ground, for in themselves they have no power.

49. Cf. Leibrecht's suggestion that this is the case, "The Life and Mind of Paul Tillich," *Religion and Culture,* p. 26.

They must be reconciled through the manifestation of the New Being, the unity of finitude and being-itself under the conditions of independent existence. Estrangement, like nonbeing, must be overcome by the power of being.

We might now compare Tillich's concept of the divine life with Fromm's concept of nature. On the basis of the preceding analyses it would seem correct to identify Tillich's concept of the self-relatedness of being as the essential difference between the two concepts. Tillich seems to hold, against such naturalists as Fromm, that nature as conceived by man is dead, the object which is merely object, the opposite, and therefore not the source, of subjectivity. According to his analysis, then, subjectivity, self-transcendence, and freedom cannot arise out of objective nature. The true source of these qualities must transcend subjectivity and objectivity, not as a lifeless identity, but by possessing them both, at least symbolically. Thus the original separation which becomes alienation is not, for Tillich, the separation of subject from object, but is the separation of life, which combines subjectivity and objectivity (and is hence self-related), from the divine life, which is likewise self-related. As a result, freedom arises from freedom, self-transcendence from self-transcendence. The divine life cannot be rationally grasped, for to conceive it is to bring it within the subject-object relationship. Such concepts as Fromm's nature ara actually symbols for the power of being-itself, viewed as Life.

There is, however, an ambiguity in Tillich's formulation. The above critique of naturalism would appear to assume that the life of the source, of being-itself, is complete of itself, apart from its creatures which are separated from it. Being-itself must be self-related in order to be the basis for self-relatedness in the creature. According to this formulation, self-relatedness separates itself from self-relatedness. Alienation is the separation of life from life.

Tillich indeed speaks, as we have seen, of separation and reunion within the divine life, both in terms of the trinitarian distinctions, and in terms of the "finite forms" created within the divine life. The reunion, as love, within the divine life implies that the divine life is eternally completed and fulfilled in itself.

According to this approach, the divine life would not be affected by the separation of the creatures from the divine life.

On the other hand, Tillich also speaks as if there were but one movement of life. As we have shown, he seems to hold predominantly that the divine life is realized *through* the separation of the creatures from the Ground. This view appears in at least two of Tillich's assertions. First, he holds, as we have seen, that divine and human freedom and self-transcendence are identical. This means that God transcends himself through human self-transcendence. Secondly, Tillich holds that the divine love is fulfilled through God's love for the creatures which are separated from him. The divine reunion with himself is at the same time the reunion of the world with its Ground. And this view would seem to be confirmed in the concluding section of the *Systematic Theology,* where Tillich observes that there can be but one process of eternal life, namely that in God. The life of the creature is a part of God's life.[50]

These two interpretations of the divine life and its relation to creatures have significantly different implications. The separation *within* life of the self-which-relates and the self-which-is-related is not a separation of life *from* life, for life contains both poles. Life transcending itself is not the same as life separated from life. Expressed in terms of human experience, the separation of subject from object is not the separation of life (combining subjectivity and objectivity) from life. Thus if there is only one movement of life, the divine life fulfilling itself through creaturely freedom and reunion through love of the creature, then the creature is only a part of life (that which goes out from itself). To put it differently, the creature is separate from life only through its subjectivity. The creature, insofar as he is free or self-transcending is God's self-transcendence, his subjectivity. In this formulation, human subjectivity becomes the transcending, and the alienating, factor.

It would seem, then, that the identification of human freedom and self-transcendence with divine freedom and self-transcend-

50. Tillich, *Systematic Theology,* III, p. 420.

ence would necessitate a return to the naturalistic position represented by Fromm. That is, alienation is a separation within life (of the self-which-relates from the self-which-is-related, of subject from object), rather than a separation of life from life. Since this movement occurs, in any case, through man, viewing it as a divine rather than human alienation and reconciliation makes no fundamental difference.

It would appear that Tillich attempts to maintain both of these views of the divine life and its relation to the creature, as in this passage cited in part above:

Where the relation of the trinitarian *personae* is described in terms of love (*amans, amatus, amor*—Augustine), it is a statement about God loving himself. The trinitarian distinctions (separation and reunion) make it possible to speak of divine self-love. Without separation from one's self, self-love is impossible. This is even more obvious, if the distinction within God includes the infinity of finite forms, which are separated and reunited in the eternal process of the divine life. The divine life is the divine self-love. Through the separation *within* himself God loves himself. And through separation *from* himself (in creaturely freedom) God fulfills his love of himself—primarily because he loves that which is estranged from himself.[51]

It would seem that Tillich here, as elsewhere, seeks to distinguish two types of divine self-love. This distinction involves two different views of the divine life. The divine life is viewed both as complete in itself, and completed through the reconciliation of the creature. Tillich has indicated that the concept of the divine life must be viewed as a symbol; but it would appear that here we have two different, and possibly conflicting, symbols for the divine life.

It was pointed out in the previous chapter that according to Tillich's own statement it is the reality of finite freedom which makes pantheism impossible. This is presumably true for Tillich because freedom implies a degree of ontological separation and independence on the part of the creature. We have noted, however, that Tillich in certain expressions equates human and divine

51. Tillich, *Systematic Theology*, I, p. 282.

self-transcendence and freedom. The question must be raised whether in this case the ontological independence disappears. Our present analysis has brought us essentially to the same point. To the extent that Tillich views the divine life as complete apart from the creature, the divine freedom and self-transcendence cannot be identified with that of the creature; but to the extent that the divine life is fulfilled through the life of the creature, divine and human freedom can be equated. We have sought to show that this second theme is certainly present, and is perhaps dominant, in Tillich's thought. If this is true, however, the claim that human freedom requires a full ontological independence on the part of the creature cannot be maintained.

If all estrangement is ultimately self-estrangement, in Tillich's view, and our analysis has sought to show that this is the case, then the conclusion that the world is viewed by Tillich as an aspect of the divine life is inescapable. All separation is separation within the divine life. More exactly, that which goes out from the divine life is an aspect of the divine life (its own self-transcendence). Thus far, we might say that pantheism has not been avoided.

The meaning of the assertion that for Tillich the world is an aspect of the divine life must be further examined, however, before the conclusion can be drawn that this view means for Tillich what it means for pantheism. Does this position mean for Tillich that finite individuality is separate from the divine life only through estrangement? Or does it mean that it is good only when it is merged with the divine? We may recall that Fromm was criticized for failing to give individuality a basis other than estrangement. Is the same in fact true for Tillich? Is individuality an evil which is eliminated through reunion? (Fromm, of course, does not hold this view; but he does not adequately protect his thought against it.)

Tillich, as we have seen, speaks at times of the divine life as self-separating and self-returning, with the implication that separation is overcome and eliminated through reunion. However, this is not his real intention. We are brought back here to the meaning which Tillich gives to the concepts of life and love. For

Tillich, as for Hegel, life is "the union of union and nonunion."[52] Both separation and union are necessary if life is to be fulfilled through love. We have seen that separation is only completed in individualization "outside" the divine life (which in another sense is a part of the divine life). Reunion for Tillich, however, as we shall now seek to show, is not a return to the unity of the ground of being; rather, it is a union which preserves the complete separation. Finite individualization is affirmed, even in reunion.

In Tillich's thought, this affirmation of finite individualization is only partially revealed in his treatment of love. As we have seen, his basic understanding of love is "the drive toward the reunion of the separated." This formula, however, could mean the reabsorption of the finite in the ground of being. In one of his discussions of love Tillich states his position more explicitly.

The ontology of love is tested by the experience of love fulfilled. There is a profound ambiguity about this experience. Fulfilled love is, at the same time, extreme happiness and the end of happiness. The separation is overcome. But without the separation there is no love and no life. It is the superiority of the person-to-person relationship that it preserves the separation of the self-centered self, and nevertheless actualizes their reunion in love. The highest form of love and that form of it which distinguishes Eastern and Western cultures is the love which preserves the individual who is both the subject and the object of love. In the loving person-to-person relationship Christianity manifests its superiority to any other religious tradition.[53]

This passage, though somewhat ambiguous, suggests that separation is preserved in the reunion of love between persons; but the passage does not indicate how this is applied to love between man and God. Tillich's discussions of love in the *Systematic Theology* indicate that separation is necessary for life and love but do not clearly indicate how separation is both preserved and overcome in love.[54]

52. Hegel, "Fragment of a System," in *On Christianity* . . . , p. 312.
53. Tillich, *Love, Power, and Justice*, p. 27.
54. Cf. Tillich, *Systematic Theology*, I, pp. 279–280; *Systematic Theology*, II, p. 47; *Systematic Theology*, III, pp. 134–138, 413.

The necessity for preserving finite individualization is more substantially established by Tillich in two related concepts: that of reconciled man or the New Being, and that of ecstasy. The New Being does not, for Tillich, take the form of a return to the unity of the Ground. On the contrary, as we have seen, the ground of being, in condescension, "enters" finite existence and thus reconciles it with itself, while preserving finite individuality.[55] The dialectical movement of separation and return is broken; in reunion, the separation remains. This means that the union with God achieved through love does not require the sacrifice of individuality. The entrance of being-itself into finite existence is paradoxical, but in this formulation the goodness of finite individuality is affirmed. This theme of divine grace fulfilling rather than negating finite individuality must be strongly emphasized. Tillich's Christology and his understanding of the New Being require a distinction between actualized individuality and estrangement. In the New Being, man's essential individuality and freedom are actualized without estrangement.

The state of fragmentary reunion with the Divine Spirit is viewed by Tillich as a state of "ecstasy." In this condition, the structures of finite existence are preserved; yet at the same time one is elevated beyond them in a "successful self-transcendence." The presence of the Divine Spirit elevates the individual above his self-relatedness, but the finite order is not thereby destroyed. "Religiously speaking, God does not need to destroy his created world, which is good in its essential nature, in order to manifest himself in it."[56]

We conclude, then, that although Tillich does not preserve a genuine ontological independence of the world over against God's being and life, he does, in his concepts of New Being and of ecstasy, preserve the goodness of separate, finite individuality. God's life is fulfilled through the creature; this theme might be identified as a pantheistic element in his thought. But this fulfillment requires that creatures exist in independence "outside" of

---

55. Cf. Tillich, *Systematic Theology*, II, pp. 94–96.
56. Tillich, *Systematic Theology*, III, p. 114.

the divine life. Thus finite separation is good so long as it exists in union with the ground of being through love. It might be said that Tillich's thought sustains a tension between pantheistic elements and the more orthodox position that finitude is good even in separation from the divine life.

summary
and conclusions

As was suggested in Chapter One, the purpose of this study has been twofold: to examine Tillich's method of correlation by actually attempting to use it in relation to the analysis of human existence formulated by Fromm and to examine the idea of alienation or estrangement in its historical development and in its usage by Fromm and Tillich. We find that these two areas are, in fact, interrelated; Tillich's method of correlation is based upon his understanding of the nature of estrangement. By seeking to show how Tillich's theological method might be applied to Fromm's thought, a critique of Fromm's concept of alienation has been carried out; at the same time, a comparison of Tillich's concept of estrangement with Fromm's naturalistic version of the same concept provides a perspective for a critique of the theological adequacy of Tillich's formulation. We are now in a position to summarize our conclusions.

We have been concerned in our study of Tillich primarily with three areas of correlation: the ontological analysis of essential finitude in correlation with the theological understanding of God, being-itself or the power of being; the existential analysis of estrangement in correlation with the theological understanding of the creation, the fall, and the New Being; and the analysis of the ambiguities of life by various philosophers of process in correlation with the theological understanding of the Divine Spirit, or unambiguous life. In our effort to determine the meaning of estrangement, we have focused more specifically upon the separation of essence and existence and their possible reunion. The doctrine of creation proves to be the bridge between the ontological analysis of finitude and the existential awareness of estrangement. Finitude remains a question mark until essential finitude is understood theologically as finitude-in-unity-with-being-itself. The estrangement of existence from essence can then be understood as the estrangement of finitude from its unity with being-itself. Thus, if our analysis is correct, the primary separation in Tillich's thought, which makes the method of correlation possible, is the estrangement of man-in-his-world from being-itself, understood as a self-estrangement. The analysis of finitude undertaken by philosophy leads in two directions: to the quest for being-itself, in the light of which finitude can be understood; and to the recognition that actual existence is a distortion of true finitude, and hence to the quest for the New Being.

The primary focus of our study has been upon the possibility of correlation between the existential analysis of estrangement and the theological answers. We first sought to establish that Tillich's method actually consists of a form of "elevation" of existentialist ideas of estrangement and reconciliation, achieved by the application of the criterion of self-estrangement. That is, if estrangement can be shown to be total, an estrangement of man-in-his-world, then the only answer possible is the answer which comes to man from beyond his existence. Tillich seems at times to assume that all existentialists view man's existence as totally estranged; however, he also concedes that this is not the case and makes implicit or explicit use of the criterion of self-estrangement as an instrument of the theological critique of existentialist views of estrangement. We suggested that existentialism approached in this way may serve as a kind of natural anthropology for Tillich's theology.

Turning to the thought of Fromm, we showed that he can be viewed as an existentialist in the sense in which Tillich uses the term. Indeed, though Fromm stands in the psychoanalytic tradition he has received a decisive influence from Karl Marx, especially the Hegelian elements in Marx. Fromm views man as emerging out of the natural harmonies through the advent of self-consciousness. The consequent separation from nature produces an alienation, a painful loneliness and sense of isolation, hence a sense of powerlessness. Nevertheless, Fromm views this alienation as potentially a progressive step. If man can move forward to a full consciousness of all aspects of nature (through "making the unconscious conscious"), he will become reunited with nature, his fellow man, and himself, now on a mature level. Indeed, reconciliation is viewed optimistically as the completion of the process which led to alienation in its initiation (the achievement of self-consciousness).

Having Fromm's view of alienation before us, we turned to the question of whether Fromm's description constitutes a self-alienation. We concluded that Fromm describes, rather, the alienation of the *ego,* or conscious self, from the non*ego,* or unconscious self, the subjective from the nonsubjective. This is a separation *within* the totality of the self, rather than an alienation of the self viewed as a totality. Man moves from a primal, unconscious harmony, through partial consciousness, to full consciousness where man is reunited with the All. Though this movement requires a social development, there is nothing inherent in man which prevents his reconciling himself through social and psychological growth toward maturity.

An attempt was then made to show how Fromm's formulation might be pressed to the point where estrangement becomes self-estrangement. The question was raised whether lonely isolation is the only form of alienation. It was pointed out that Fromm sees the danger of regressive reunion, which is, in his thought, both a form of alienation and an escape from alienation. If alienation includes regression, then it can no longer be viewed as a progressive step, and Fromm's evolutionary scheme is weakened. It was shown that Tillich might effectively argue that both submergence (or regression) and isolation are forms of alienation and that one drives toward the other. Loneliness breeds submergence, and vice versa. This empirical observation, Tillich might maintain, necessitates a refinement in the understanding of alienation. Not only man's individuality (in whatever form), but also his participation (in whatever form) has become estranged; indeed, when one is estranged, so is the other, for they are polar characteristics in man. Man's separateness as such is not alienation, for he may be separate and a participant at the same time. In fact, it is of man's essence that he is the one because he is the other.

Tillich maintains that it is that complex entity known as the self which becomes estranged. The self has a world which it is in; it is both individual and participant; it is self-related. If proper or essential separation (solitude) becomes isolation, then proper or essential participation (communion) becomes submergence (or domination by the nonsubjective). If the *ego*-self is estranged, the world which it has, and is in, is also estranged; if consciousness is estranged, the unconscious is also estranged. Estrangement is not the separation of subject from object; this separation is rooted in the self-relatedness of being. The separation described as estrangement must be a separation of the self-in-its-world from its essential nature, rather than a separation *within* the self.

If the estrangement of the self is total, if the existence of the self-in-its-world is estranged, then that from which the self is estranged, and with which it must be reconciled, must be beyond existence. But if estrangement is self-estrangement, then that from which the self is separated must be, in some sense, identical with the self. Our analysis has sought to show how Tillich uses the "symbols of the Christian message," in both a mythological and an ontological form, to explain how man has become self-estranged, and may become reconciled. Tillich's analysis is rooted in his understanding of the divine as "life." Like all life, the divine has, according to Tillich, the characteristic of going out from itself in self-transcendence and creativity and returning to itself through love. The divine life is eternally creative, creating finite forms "within itself" in "inexhaustible abundance." The mythological Adam and the ontological concept of finitude-in-unity-with-being-itself point to the reality of finitude within the divine life.

According to Tillich, finitude, in the power of being-itself, sustains itself against the threat of nonbeing through self-transcendence. Though characteristic of all finite being (and, symbolically, of being-itself), the process of self-transcendence reaches the point in man of self-consciousness and of finite freedom. Here the creature reaches the point of going out from its unity with the divine life. Since self-consciousness and freedom are involved, this act of separation must be chosen and affirmed consciously. It is not only an ontological movement, it is also a free decision. The actualization of finite freedom in the power of the divine life separates the creature from the divine life, and thus from its own essential finitude, in estranged existence. This existence, however, is at the same time full individualization (through self-consciousness) and is, as such, the completion of creation—the completion of the drive of being toward the greatest individualization and separation. This situation of estrangement is represented by the mythological doctrine of the fall of man and by the existentialist analysis of the separation of essence and existence (under the theological criterion).

Reconciliation, as Tillich understands it, is the reunion of existence with essential finitude, which means the reunion of existence with finitude-in-unity-with-being-itself. This, for Tillich, is not an evolutionary movement where alienation reaches its culmination in reconciliation. Reconciliation is rather the manifestation of finitude-in-unity-with-being-itself under the conditions of estranged existence. This manifestation is fragmentarily found in all human history and is fulfilled, according to Christian theology, in the New Being manifest in Jesus as the Christ. Here, in a concrete historical event, salvation and reconciliation appear in the manifestation of the eternal God-manhood, or finitude-in-unity-with-being-itself under the conditions of existence. This actualization is not just a restoration of essential finitude; it combines the essential with "the positive which is created within existence."

What conclusions can be drawn from this comparison of the thought of Fromm and Tillich? We might first consider the critique of Fromm's analysis of alienation. We conclude that the Tillichian criticism of Fromm's naturalistic version is basically sound. It seems legitimate to maintain that man, if alienated at all, is alienated as both individual and participant. Man is a unity, even in alienation. Hence, on the one hand, Fromm's concept of man's primal (and teleological) nature ought to provide a more secure foundation for man's individuality; and, on the other hand, man's alienation must be more nearly complete than Fromm recognizes. We conclude that Tillich's description of the self as essentially both individual and participant provides a more nearly adequate basis for interpreting the data of estrangement, i.e., that man is estranged both from proper individuality and proper participation. On the level of the concept of selfhood and its estrangement we would thus be inclined to accept Tillich's analysis. Fromm does not present an adequate picture of the total self-in-its-world.

Two points concerning Tillich's relation to Fromm's naturalism require further comment. The first is that Tillich seeks an ontological foundation for the self and its freedom, while Fromm confines himself largely to a history of consciousness (combined with a semiscientific concept of the essential nature of man). Tillich's position in relation to that of Fromm is somewhat similar to the view adopted by Marx in relation to Hegel and Feuerbach. For Marx, alienation occurs in "real life"; alienation in consciousness is only a reflection of the real-life situation. It is true that in Marx's view man through his "activity" constitutes his world either as an alienated or as a reconciled world, but activity for Marx is more than consciousness.

Similarly, for Tillich, estrangement in consciousness is a reflection of estrangement in being. The self in its totality is estranged, not just in its consciousness. This view in Tillich's thought hinges on the understanding of human freedom, or free activity, as a movement in being (a separation from the Ground), not just a state of consciousness. Tillich, indeed, views this movement as a general structure of reality, the "self-relatedness of being," which is brought to fruition in man. Man is truly a microcosm for Tillich, even in his self-consciousness or self-relatedness. Perhaps Tillich's critique of Fromm might be summed up in this fashion: if man by becoming "subject" has become basically alien to nature, the objective world, then he cannot be reconciled with it. Only if man in his self-relatedness is rooted in the self-relatedness of being can he be reconciled. Man's self-relatedness cannot be derived from, nor reconciled with, objective nature. The power of man's being comes from being-itself, which is itself self-related, which is itself eternal life, combining subjectivity and objectivity.

This is an impressive, closely reasoned critique of naturalism. However, it raises an important issue concerning the relation of the divine life to finite life in Tillich's account. The question is this: is God's life in Tillich's view complete in itself or completed only through the life of the creature?

We have maintained that Tillich predominantly gives the latter answer. Let us review some of the consequences of this position. In this point of view, creaturely self-transcendence and freedom *is* the divine self-transcendence and freedom. And creaturely reconciliation with the Creator is the divine self-reconciliation. God thus creates himself through his creation of the world and reconciles himself through his reconciliation with the world. Here there is but one Life, poured into finitude, and transcending itself through human freedom.

This means, however, that the separation is within Life, rather than between the divine life and finite life. Speaking symbolically, man's subjectivity is God's subjectivity. On the level of the divine life, it would appear that self-estrangement must be conceptualized as the separation of "subject" and "object," the separation of the self-which-transcends from the self-which-is-transcended. On the other hand, our analysis has shown that on the finite level Tillich does not consider the separation of subject and object to be the primary estrangement; and the naturalist view has been criticized for understanding estrangement as the subject-object split. Does Tillich reinstate on the divine level what he has rejected on the finite level? Does Tillich break with reductionist naturalism only to reinstate a "self-transcending" naturalism?

With regard to the most prominent aspects of Tillich's analysis this question must be answered affirmatively. We have noted, however, that another form of dialectical process appears to be involved in the manifestation of the holy within existence and in the achievement of ecstacy. Here the power of the Divine Spirit is conceived as entering finitude, elevating the finite beyond its self-relatedness, beyond subjectivity and objectivity. This entrance is, in Tillich's view, grace, not nature. But this means that the divine is free in relation to the world in a form other than man's freedom. It means that the divine power can enter the finite in a form other than that of "natural" self-transcendence; and this would seem to imply that the divine life is in some sense independent of and complete apart from the life of the creature.

It would appear that this relationship could be symbolized in Tillich's categories by referring to finite life as created "in the image" of the divine life, as empowered by the divine life to transcend itself, but in some sense an independent life, possessing its own separate subjectivity and objectivity. The resulting position would preserve the concept of estrangement as the separation of life (combining subjectivity and objectivity) from the unambiguous divine life. It appears that this view would provide a more effective critique of naturalism. However, this formulation breaks the continuity between the divine life and human life which forms the basis for the dialectical structure of self-estrangement.

If this modification is rejected (as it probably would be by Tillich) the alternative is to speak honestly of Tillich's system as a self-transcending naturalism. Since this is a new form of naturalism (one might question the use of the term at all), it cannot be viewed as necessarily inadequate for an expression of the Christian world-view. It is, however, clearly in conflict with traditional theism (which Tillich calls supernaturalism). Tillich's rejection of supernaturalism suggests a reconsideration on the part of Christian theology of its relation to various types of humanistic naturalism. Tillich has certainly made clear his view that the existence of a supernatural being is not the real foundation for Christian theology. This writer is in sympathy with the call for a reappraisal at this point, although it need not be assumed that Tillich has the last word on the subject.

Our second observation concerns the progressive, utopian aspect of Fromm's thought. Is Tillich's scheme really progressive and utopian also? It *is* possible to say for Tillich, as for Fromm, that the "fall' is also an advance, that it has a progressive aspect. Here, however, the similarity stops. For Tillich, the power of life which produces self-transcendence and alienation cannot of itself achieve reconciliation. Finite life is tragic; its greatness leads inevitably to its own disruption. Only the holy, the ecstatic, is beyond tragedy; this appears only when the world constituted by the subject-object split is "overcome."

Tillich therefore foresees no progressive realization of reconciled existence but only its fragmentary manifestation in moments of grace. His view of history is one of tragedy. Only those fragmentary moments of elevation beyond history are beyond tragedy. These moments do, however, in another sense, appear within history, but not in a progressive fashion. Christianity, with "daring faith," finds the full achievement of ecstatic reconciliation in the person of Christ. Here is provided a center and a criterion for the New Being within existence. But the beginning (essential finitude) and the end ("essentialization" in the Kingdom of God) are mythological-eschatological; life does not develop progressively from the one to the other. Here one finds a distinct parting of the ways for the theologian and the naturalistic-humanist on the matter of interpreting human history. This writer finds more realism in the Tillichian view, but the restraint which this view exhibits concerning human potentialities requires perennial challenge from the side of Fromm's chastened optimism.

A word may now be said about the achievement of each writer. Fromm's major accomplishment would appear to be his analysis of the nature of human consciousness. Fromm illuminates the fact that man's self-awareness has its own history, rooted, to be sure, in the physical organism, but transcending it and going through its own process of development. Furthermore, the primary determining forces in this development are not understood to be the physiological drives but rather the social forces which shape conscious awareness. Fromm's major contribution appears in his delineation of the ways in which society, in the very act of fostering individual awareness, restricts the content of consciousness, thus alienating man from the fullness of his humanity. In this analysis, Fromm unites the Marxian concepts of ideology and false consciousness with the psychoanalytic ideas of rationalization and repression. This interweaving of two major intellectual traditions is an accomplishment of considerable importance.

With regard to Tillich, the great achievement of any comprehensive "system" is that of synthesis: the discovery of continuities and relationships among diverse regions of reality and diverse areas of human thought and action. Who can doubt that this is one of the essential functions of the intellect (though not perhaps the only one)? Tillich's achievement in this regard is undeniable. His system, for example, reverses the trend, characteristic of both liberalism and Neo-orthodoxy, toward a radical cleavage between man and nature. Rather, he sees human existence as the fulfillment of the drive of nature (indeed of all being) toward individualization and self-relatedness. This systematic construction brings Tillich's thought into contact with the sciences of physics and biology, as well as psychology and sociology. (Incidentally, the evaluation of the system is consequently not solely a theological and philosophical matter but involves physical, biological, and socio-psychological questions.)

Similarly, Tillich attempts to discover a positive relationship between religion and culture. His standpoint as a Christian in relation to culture is conversionist rather than exclusivistic. As a result, Tillich can enter into appreciative dialogue with a wide variety of concerns manifested in modern culture: existentialism, psychoanalysis, modern art, non-Western religions, secular religions (such as Marxism), Western secular humanism, etc. (It is perhaps this aspect of Tillich's synoptic vision which is most responsible for the wide interest which his thought has provoked.)

Surely it is a daring enterprise which Tillich has undertaken, and one can only say that the product is vastly provocative. In this writer's opinion, those who argue (from the standpoint of linguistic analysis) that certain of Tillich's central categories are meaningless are refuted by the fact that a distinct world-view emerges from the pages of the *Systematic Theology*. Tillich presents a recognizable vision of reality with which one can come to grips with either a positive or a negative response. But the vision is there—a vision thoroughly steeped in the Christian and the Western metaphysical traditions. Tillich's contribution to constructive Christian thinking is unsurpassed in our time.

We must now conclude. Hopefully this comparative study has shed some light upon the two perspectives. And perhaps in some small way we can claim more than this: an illumination of certain aspects of man's universal predicament.

BIBLIOGRAphy

ALSTON, WILLIAM P. "Tillich on Idolatry," *Journal of Religion,* XXXVIII (October, 1958), pp. 263–268.

ANSHEN, RUTH NANDA (ed.). *The Family: Its Function and Destiny.* New York: Harper, 1949.

————(ed.). *Freedom: Its Meaning.* ("Science of Culture Series," Vol. I) New York: Harcourt Brace and Co., 1940.

————(ed.). *Moral Principles of Action.* ("Science of Culture Series," Vol. VI) New York: Harper, 1952.

AULÉN, GUSTAF. *The Faith of the Christian Church.* Philadelphia: The Muhlenberg Press, 1948.

BASILIUS, HAROLD A. (ed.). *Contemporary Problems in Religion.* Detroit: Wayne University Press, 1956.

BLUM, GERALD S. *Psychoanalytic Theories of Personality.* New York: McGraw Hill, 1953.

BRUNNER, HEINRICH EMIL. *Man in Revolt.* Translated by Olive Wyon. New York: Charles Scribner's Sons, 1939.

DEWEY, JOHN. *A Common Faith.* New Haven: Yale University Press, 1934.

EDIE, JAMES M. (ed.). *What Is Phenomenology?* Chicago: Quadrangle Books, 1962.

FERRÉ, NELS F. S. *The Christian Understanding of God.* New York: Harper and Brothers, 1951.

FEUER, LEWIS S. (ed.). *Marx and Engels, Basic Writings on Politics and Philosophy.* Anchor Books. Garden City: Doubleday Anchor and Co., Inc., 1959.

FEUERBACH, LUDWIG ANDREAS. *The Essence of Christianity.* Translated by George Eliot, with an Introduction by Karl Barth, foreword by H. Richard Niebuhr. New York: Harper Torchbook, Harper and Brothers, 1957.

FREUD, SIGMUND. *Civilization and Its Discontents.* Translated by Joan Riviere. London: Hogarth Press Ltd., 1953.

183

———. *The Future of an Illusion.* Translated by W. D. Robson-Scott. Garden City: Doubleday and Co., Inc., Doubleday Anchor Books, 1957.

———. *A General Introduction to Psychoanalysis.* Translated in the revised edition by Joan Riviere. Garden City: Garden City Books, 1952.

FROMM, ERICH. *The Art of Loving.* New York: Harper, 1956.

———. *Beyond the Chains of Illusion.* New York: A Trident Press Book, Simon and Schuster, 1962.

———. "Die Entwicklung des Christusdogmas," *Imago, Zeitschrift für Anwendung der Psychoanalyse auf die Natur- und Geisteswissenschaften,* XVI (Heft 3/4, 1930), pp. 305–373.

———. "Die Psychoanalytische Charaktologie und ihre Bedeutung für die Sozialpsychologie," *Zeitschrift für Sozialforschung,* I (Heft 3, 1932), pp. 253–277.

———. *The Dogma of Christ.* New York: Holt, Rinehart and Winston, 1963.

———. *Escape from Freedom.* New York: Rinehart, 1941.

———. "Faith as a Character Trait," *Psychiatry,* V (August, 1942), pp. 307–319.

———. *The Forgotten Language.* New York: Rinehart, 1951.

———. "Freud and Jung," *Pastoral Psychology,* I, No. 7 (1950), pp. 11–15.

———. *The Heart of Man.* New York: Harper and Row, 1964.

———. "Individual and Social Origins of Neurosis," *American Sociological Review,* IX (August, 1944), pp. 380–384.

———. "Love and Its Disintegration," *Pastoral Psychology,* VII, No. 68 (1956), pp. 37–44.

———. "Man Is Not a Thing," *Saturday Review,* XL (March 16, 1957), pp. 9–11.

———. *Man for Himself.* New York: Rinehart, 1947.

———. *Marx's Concept of Man.* New York: Frederick Ungar Publishing Co., 1961.

———. *May Man Prevail?* Garden City: Doubleday and Co., Inc., Doubleday Anchor Books, 1961.

———. "Present Human Condition," *The American Scholar,* XXV (Winter, 1955), pp. 29–35.

———. *Psychoanalysis and Religion.* New Haven: Yale University Press, 1950.

———. *The Sane Society.* New York: Rinehart, 1955.

————. *Sigmund Freud's Mission.* 1st ed. New York: Harper, 1959.

————. "The Social Philosophy of 'Will Therapy,' " *Psychiatry,* II (May, 1939), pp. 230–233.

————. "Über Methode und Aufgabe einer analytischen Sozial-psychologie," *Zeitschrift für Sozialforschung,* I (Doppelheft 1/2, 1932), pp. 28–54.

————, D. T. SUZUKI, and RICHARD DE MARTINO. *Zen Buddhism and Psychoanalysis.* New York: Harper and Bros., 1960.

GABUS, JEAN-PAUL. "Un Grand Théologien: Paul Tillich," *Foi et Vie,* 6 (November–December 1960), pp. 432–444.

HAMILTON, KENNETH. *The System and the Gospel.* New York: The Macmillan Co., 1963.

HARTSHORNE, CHARLES. *The Divine Relativity.* New Haven: Yale University Press, 1948.

HEGEL, GEORGE WILHELM FRIEDRICH. *Early Theological Writings.* Translated by T. M. Knox, with an Introduction and fragments translated by Richard Kroner, Chicago: University of Chicago Press, 1948.

————. *The Phenomenology of Mind.* Translated with an Introduction and notes, J. B. Baillie. Second edition revised and corrected throughout. New York: Macmillan, 1931.

————. *Selections.* Ed. J. Loewenberg. New York: Charles Scribner's Sons, 1929.

HEIDEGGER, MARTIN. *Kant and the Problem of Metaphysics.* Translated with an Introduction by James S. Churchill. Bloomington, Indiana: Indiana University Press, 1962.

HEINEMANN, F. H. *Existentialism and the Modern Predicament.* New York: Harper and Bros., 1953.

HERBERG, WILL. "Religion and Social Reality," *Commentary* (March, 1957), pp. 277–284.

————. "Riesman's Lonely Man," *Commonweal,* LX (September 3, 1954), pp. 538–540.

HOOK, SIDNEY. *The Quest for Being.* New York: St. Martin's Press, 1961.

———— (ed.). *Religious Experience and Truth: A Symposium.* New York: New York University Press, 1961.

HORNEY, KAREN. *The Neurotic Personality of Our Time.* New York: W. W. Norton and Co., Inc., 1937.

HORTON, WALTER MARSHALL. *Christian Theology: An Ecumenical*

Approach. New York: Harper and Bros., 1955.

KARIEL, H. S. "The Normative Pattern of Fromm's Escape from Freedom," *Journal of Politics,* XIX (November, 1957), pp. 640–654.

KASCH, WILHELM F. "Die Lehre von der Inkarnation in der Theologie Paul Tillichs," *Zeitschrift für Theologie und Kirche,* (April, 1961), pp. 86–103.

KECKEMETI, PAUL. "The All-Powerful 'I,' " *Commentary,* XXI (February, 1956), pp. 176–179.

KEGLEY, CHARLES W. and ROBERT W. BRETALL (eds.). *The Theology of Paul Tillich.* New York: Macmillan, 1952.

KIERKEGAARD, SOREN. *The Sickness unto Death.* New York: Doubleday and Co., Inc., Doubleday Anchor Books, 1954.

KRIKORIAN, YERVANT H. (ed.). *Naturalism and the Human Spirit.* New York: Columbia University Press, 1944.

LAM, E. P. "Tillich's Reconstruction of the Concept of Ideology," *Christianity and Society,* VI (Winter, 1940), pp. 11–15.

LEIBRECHT, WALTER (ed.). *Religion and Culture: Essays in Honor of Paul Tillich.* New York: Harper and Bros., 1959.

LEVI, ALBERT W. *Philosophy and the Modern World.* Bloomington, Indiana: Indiana University Press, 1959.

MACKINTOSH, HUGH ROSS. *Types of Modern Theology.* London: Nisbet and Co., Ltd., 1952.

MARCUSE, HERBERT. *Eros and Civilization.* Boston: Beacon Press, 1955.

———. *Reason and Revolution: Hegel and the Rise of Social Theory.* London: Routledge and Kegan Paul, Ltd., 1955.

MARX, KARL. *Capital.* Vol. I. Ed. Friedrich Engels. Translated by Samuel Moore and Edward Aveling. London: William Glaisher, Ltd., 1918.

———. *Karl Marx: Selected Writings in Sociology and Social Philosophy.* Ed. T. B. Bottomore and Maximilien Rubel. London: Watts and Co., 1961.

MAY, ROLLO. *The Meaning of Anxiety.* New York: Ronald Press Co., 1950.

MAY, ROLLO, ERNEST ANGEL, and HENRI F. ELLENBERGER (eds.). *Existence.* New York: Basic Books, 1958.

McCLELLAND, DAVID C. "Religious Overtones in Psychoanalysis," *Theology Today,* XVI (April, 1959), pp. 40–69.

MILLS, C. F., and HANS GERTH. *Character and the Social Structure.* New York: Harcourt, Brace and Co., 1953.

NIEBUHR, REINHOLD. Review of *Man for Himself,* by Erich Fromm, *Christianity and Society,* XIII (Spring, 1948), pp. 26–28.

NELSON, BENJAMIN (ed.). *Freud and the 20th Century.* New York: Meridian Books, Inc., 1957.

PETUCHOWSKI, JAKOB J. "Fromm's Midrash on Love," *Commentary,* XXII (December, 1956), pp. 543–549.

RANDALL, JOHN HERMAN, JR. *The Role of Knowledge in Western Religion.* Boston: Starr King Press, 1958.

RICKMAN, JOHN (ed.). *A General Selection from the Works of Sigmund Freud.* Garden City: Doubleday and Co., Doubleday Anchor Books, 1957.

RIESMAN, DAVID. "Psychological Types and National Character," *American Quarterly,* V (Winter, 1953), pp. 325–344.

ROBERTS, DAVID E. "Theological and Psychiatric Interpretations of Human Nature," *Christianity and Crisis,* VII (February 3, 1947), pp. 3–7.

SARGENT, S. STANSFIELD and MARIAN W. SMITH. *Culture and Personality.* New York: Viking Fund, 1949.

SCHAAR, JOHN H. *Escape from Authority.* New York: Basic Books, Inc., 1961.

SCHELLING, FRIEDRICH W. J. VON. *The Ages of the World.* Translated with an Introduction and notes by Frederick de Wolfe Bolman, Jr. New York: Columbia University Press, 1942.

———. *Of Human Freedom.* Translated with an Introduction by James Gutmann. Chicago: The Open Court Publishing Co., 1936.

SCHLEIERMACHER, FRIEDRICH. *The Christian Faith.* Translated by D. M. Baillie *et al.* Ed. H. R. Mackintosh and J. S. Stewart. Edinburgh: T. & T. Clark, 1928.

TAVARD, GEORGE H. *Paul Tillich and The Christian Message.* New York: Charles Scribner's Sons, 1962.

THOMAS, J. HEYWOOD. *Paul Tillich: An Appraisal.* Philadelphia: The Westminster Press, 1963.

THOMPSON, CLARA. *Psychoanalysis: Its Evolution and Development.* New York: Hermitage House, 1950.

TIEBOUT, H. M., JR. "Tillich and Freud on Sin," *Religion in Life,* XXVIII (Spring, 1959), pp. 223–235.

TILLICH, PAUL. "Beyond Religious Socialism: How My Mind Has Changed," *Christian Century,* LXVI (June 15, 1949), pp. 732–733.

———. *Christianity and the Encounter of the World Religions.* New York: Columbia University Press, 1963.

——. "The Conception of Man in Existential Philosophy," *Journal of Religion,* XIX (July, 1939), pp. 201–215.

——. *The Courage to Be.* New Haven: Yale University Press, 1952.

——. "Erich Fromm's *The Sane Society,*" *Pastoral Psychology,* VI (September, 1955), pp. 13–16.

——. "Estrangement and Reconciliation in Modern Thought," *Review of Religion,* IX (November, 1944), pp. 5–19.

——. "Existential Philosophy," *Journal of the History of Ideas,* V (January, 1944), pp. 44–70.

——. "Existential Thinking in American Theology," *Religion in Life,* X (Summer, 1941), pp. 452–456.

——. "Existentialism and Religious Socialism," *Christianity and Society,* XV (Winter, 1949), pp. 8–11.

——. "Existentialism, Psychotherapy, and the Nature of Man," *Pastoral Psychology,* XI (June, 1960), pp. 10–18.

——. *Frühe Hauptwerke: Gesammelte Werke Band I.* Stuttgart: Evangelisches Verlagswerk, 1959.

——. "The Good I Will, I Do Not," *Religion in Life,* XXVIII (Fall, 1959), pp. 539–545.

——. *A History of Christian Thought.* Second edition. Lectures recorded and edited by Peter H. John. Providence, Rhode Island: Privately multigraphed, 1956.

——. "How Much Truth Is in Karl Marx?," *Christian Century,* LXV (September, 1948), pp. 906–908.

——. "The Idea of a Personal God," *Union Review,* II (November, 1940), pp. 8–10.

——. "The Impact of Pastoral Psychology on Theological Thought," *Pastoral Psychology,* XI (February, 1960), pp. 17–23.

——. *Interpretation of History.* Part I, translated by N. A. Rasetzki; parts II, III, and IV translated by Elsa L. Talmey. New York: C. Scribner's Sons, 1936.

——. "Ist eine Wissenschaft von den Werten Möglich?" *Zeitschrift für Evangelische Ethik,* (May, 1961), pp. 171–176.

——. "Jewish Influences," *Cross Currents,* II (Spring, 1952), pp. 35–42.

——. *Love, Power and Justice.* New York: Oxford University Press, A Galaxy Book, 1960.

——. "Man and Society in Religious Socialism," *Christianity and Society,* VIII (Fall, 1943), pp. 10–21.

——. "Martin Buber and Christian Thought," *Commentary,* V (June, 1948), pp. 515–521.

————. *Morality and Beyond*. New York: Harper and Row, 1963.

————. "Natural and Revealed Religion," *Christendom*, I (October, 1935), pp. 155–171.

————. "The Nature of Man," *Journal of Philosophy*, XLIII (December 5, 1946), pp. 675–676.

————. "Nietzsche and the Bourgeois Spirit," *Journal of the History of Ideas*, VI (June, 1945), pp. 307–309.

————. "Nicholai Berdyaev," *Religion in Life*, VII (Summer, 1938), pp. 407–415.

————. "The Problem of Theological Method," *Journal of Religion*, XXVII (January, 1947), pp. 16–26.

————. *The Protestant Era*. Translated and edited by James Luther Adams. London: Nisbet and Co., Ltd., 1951.

————. "Psychoanalysis, Existentialism, and Theology," *The Christian Register*, CXXXV, (March, 1956), pp. 16–17; 34–36.

————. "Psychotherapy and a Christian Interpretation of Human Nature," *Review of Religion*, XIII (March, 1949), pp. 264–269.

————. "The Relation of Religion and Health," *Review of Religion*, X (May, 1946), pp. 348–384.

————. Review of *Psychoanalysis and Religion*, by Erich Fromm, *Pastoral Psychology*, II (June, 1951), pp. 62–66.

————. *Systematic Theology*. Vol. I. Chicago: University of Chicago Press, 1951.

————. *Systematic Theology*. Vol. II. Chicago: University of Chicago Press, 1957.

————. *Systematic Theology*. Vol. III. Chicago: University of Chicago Press, 1963.

————. *Theology of Culture*. Ed. Robert C. Kimball. New York: Oxford University Press, 1959.

————. "Vertical and Horizontal Thinking," *American Scholar*, XV (Winter, 1945), pp. 102–105.

TUCKER, ROBERT. *Philosophy and Myth in Karl Marx*. Cambridge: Cambridge University Press, 1961.

VAN DUSEN, HENRY P. (ed.). *The Christian Answer*. New York: Charles Scribner's Sons, 1945.

WILLIAMS, DANIEL DAY. *What Present-Day Theologians Are Thinking*. New York: Harper and Bros., 1952.

WINTHROP, HENRY. Review of *The Sane Society*, by Erich Fromm, *Journal of Social Psychology*, XLV (February, 1957), pp. 125–134.

index

191